D1279336

ROOKIES OF THE YEAR

LA

ROOKIES OF THE YEAR

New Kids Who Took the Field

DAVID CRAFT

MetroBooks

MetroBooks

An Imprint of Friedman/Fairfax Publishers

Library of Congress Cataloging-in-Publication Data

Craft, David.
Rookies of the year : new kids who took the field / David Craft.
p. cm.
Includes bibliographical references (p.) and index.
ISBN 1-56799-143-2
1. Rookie of the Year Award. Baseball players—United States—Biography. I. Title.
GV865.A1C68 1995
796.357'092'2—dc20
[B] 94-27732
CIP

Editor: Benjamin Boyington
Art Director: Jeff Batzli
Designers: Stan Stanski and Kevin Ullrich
Photography Editors: Susan Mettler and Wendy Missan

Color separations by Advanced Laser Graphic Arts (International) Ltd.
Printed in China by Leefung-Asco Printers Ltd.

For bulk purchases and special sales, please contact:
Friedman/Fairfax Publishers
Attention: Sales Department
15 West 26th Street
New York, NY 10010
(212) 685-6610 FAX (212) 685-1307

Photography Credits

AP/Wide World Photos: 1, 7, 10, 13, 14, 16, 18, 19 right, 20 right, 22 both, 23, 24 bottom, 25 top, 26 left, 28, 29 right, 31 right, 33 right, 34 both, 35 bottom, 37 both, 38 both, 39 both, 42 right, 43 right, 45 both, 46 right, 48 right, 51 both, 64 right, 67 top, 68 left

Archive: 25 bottom

© Bob Bartosz: 48 left

© Focus on Sports: 44, 50 left, 53 both, 55, 57 left, 60 left, 62, 64 left, 67 bottom, 68 right, 69 right, 75, 77 top; © Mickey Palmer: 49 left, 54 both; © Chuck Solomon: 56; © Jerry Wachter: 36, 43 left, 52 right

FPG International: 57 right; © Richard Mackson: 58; © Hy Peskin: 17, 19 left, 21 right, 27

National Baseball Library and Archive, Cooperstown, N.Y.: 11, 12, 20 left, 21 left, 24 right, 26 right, 29 left, 31 left, 41, 47 left

Reuters: 76 left

Sportschrome East/West: 6, 60 right, 63, 66, 69 left, 72 right; © Jeff Carlick: 70; © Vincent Manniello: 76 right; © Louis A. Raynor: 72 left, 73 left; © C. Rydlewski: 59; © Robert Tringali, Jr.: 9, 71, 73 right, 77 bottom; © Ron Wyatt: 61

Sports Illustrated: © Walter Iooss, Jr.: 46 left; © Tony Triolo: 50 right; © John G. Zimmerman: 30

Sports Photo Masters, Inc.: © Mitchell B. Reibel: 42 left, 52 left; © Don Smith: 74

© Dave Stock: 2, 3, 40, 65

UPI/Bettmann: 15, 32, 33 left, 35 top, 47 right, 49 right

Acknowledgments

I wish to thank Jack Lang, executive secretary of the Baseball Writers Association of America, and Bill Deane, author and researcher, for their information and insights essential to the writing of this book.

Dedication

This book is dedicated to the memory of Tom Alston, a Cardinals rookie in the spring of 1954 and the team's first black player. Tom once told me that he would forever be disappointed that his big-league career—which was over by 1958—never blossomed the way he had hoped or that others had predicted for him.

But to those of us who will never know the pride that comes from donning a big-league uniform or the thrill that comes from competing at baseball's highest level, Tom's .246 batting average, 14 doubles, 4 homers, 2 triples, and 34 RBI over the course of 66 games in his rookie season will always sparkle.

CONTENTS

23

INTRODUCTION

What is a rookie, anyway? There is little agreement about the word's origins, though some people have suggested that "rookie" comes from "rook"—often the last piece to be used in a chess game. However, in *Webster's Tenth New Collegiate Dictionary* it is suggested that the term may be an alternative form of the word "recruit." That is, "rookie" is military slang that over the years has come to mean "first-year" or "newcomer."

But in the realm of Major League Baseball, "rookie" has also come to suggest something else: promise. Every new season produces dozens of rookie players itching to prove that they are worthy of the expectations of success that scouts, front-office personnel, and the press have of them. For most rookies, years of amateur ball have given way to several years of professional seasoning in the minor leagues. Some rookies stay in the majors only long enough to enjoy, as the saying goes, a cup of coffee. Others, such as Luis Aparico, Willie McCovey, and Don Drysdale, forge Hall of Fame careers. Still others have careers that more closely resemble a shooting star: they display a flash of brilliance that thrills onlookers, but then they fizzle out and disappear from the scene.

After the 1940 season, the Chicago chapter of the Baseball Writers Association of America (BBWAA) established an award to recognize the game's top rookie. Cleveland's Lou Boudreau was accorded the honor that first year, and six others received this local, minimally publicized award from 1941 through 1946.

In 1947 the national organization of the BBWAA, which had by then assumed the role of selecting the year's top rookie player, chose Jackie Robinson—the man who batted, threw, and ran baseball's racial barriers into the ground—as the first nationally recognized Rookie of the Year.

The BBWAA—either the national organization or its Chicago chapter—bestowed rookie honors on only one big-league newcomer through 1948. In 1949 the BBWAA began awarding separate honors to the top rookie in each league. This system still exists today.

Beginning with the Philadelphia Phillies' Del Ennis in 1946, *The Sporting News* started naming its own Rookie of the Year. To this day, the BBWAA and *The Sporting News* continue to give seperate rookie awards. What's more, since 1957 *The Sporting News* has made a distinction between position players and pitchers by selecting a Rookie Player of the Year and a Pitcher of the Year for each league—four rookie awards from one source alone. Add to this the fact that several other sports publications annually pick their choices for the year's top rookies, and one begins to wonder just how noteworthy the Rookie of the Year Award really is.

Of these many rookie awards, it is the one given by the BBWAA that is the most well known and is the focus of this book. This is not just because this organization created the award, but because it is the BBWAA's version that the fans, the media, and the players themselves almost always refer to when the subject comes up. In fact, according to Jack Lang, executive secretary of the BBWAA, "There are agents now who are writing into contracts bonuses for some players—who aren't even on a major league roster yet—that if and when the player makes his franchise's major league roster and he is named the Rookie of the Year, he shall get *x* amount of dollars extra."

Author and researcher Bill Deane points out that voting procedures for the award have undergone several changes over the years. In 1947, for example, thirty-three baseball writers named their top five rookie candidates in order of preference, with 5 points going to a writer's No. 1 choice, 4 points to his No. 2 choice, and so on. Robinson garnered the most points (129) and won the award. For the 1948 award, forty-eight writers participated, naming a single candidate on each ballot; Alvin Dark won. In 1949 three writers from each league city (the same men who selected the Most Valuable Players) participated in the selection process. In 1961 that figure was reduced to two writers from each league city. In 1980 the BBWAA switched to a three-candidate/5-3-1 point system that is still in effect. In this system, each writer is asked to name three rookies in order of preference, giving 5 points for a first-place vote, 3 points for a second-place vote, and 1 point for a third-place vote. The maximum number of points available to a Rookie of the Year candidate in either league is 140 (14 teams per league times 2 writers from each league city times 5 points for a first-place vote).

Deane also notes that formal guidelines for determining rookie status were not created until 1957. Like the voting procedures, these guidelines have changed over the years, with the most recent ones established in 1971. To be considered a rookie, a pitcher must have pitched a total of fewer than 50 innings in any previous season or seasons; a non-pitcher must have accumulated a total of fewer than 130 at-bats in any previous season or seasons; any player must have accumulated a total of fewer than 45 days on a major league roster prior to September 1 of any previous season. (As a side note, when infielder Gregg Jefferies was with the Mets, he was eligible for the award in 1988 and 1989, but did not garner enough votes in either year to win.) Such guidelines are important not only in the award voting, but also because players need a certain amount of big-league service before they can become free agents.

What you will find in the following pages is a season-by-season look at all the young men who won Rookie of the Year honors. Most sources prefer to start with the 1947 winner because 1947 was the first year the BBWAA went national with its award. But this book includes the seven players who won the award before Jackie Robinson took home the honors. Each section is not only packed with statistics, but also filled with information about each featured player.

Rookies of the Year: New Kids Who Took the Field details the exploits of the award-winning young men who hoped (or hope) to capitalize on the promise of their college or minor league seasons. Whether you're eight years old or eighty, you're sure to find this book entertaining and informative.

It's anyone's guess what a Rookie of the Year may accomplish beyond his rookie season. The Atlanta Braves' David Justice, the 1990 National League winner, was a key factor in the Braves' winning the World Series in 1995.

C H A P T E R O N E

THE 1940s

LOU BOUDREAU—1940

A player-manager for most of his career, Lou Boudreau led by example.

Even in his later years as a broadcaster, particularly with the Chicago Cubs, Lou Boudreau was known as "Good Kid."

Because of this it seems particularly fitting that he holds the distinction of being named Major League Baseball's first Rookie of the Year, as voted by members of the Chicago chapter of the Baseball Writers' Association of America (BBWAA).

Boudreau joined the Cleveland Indians organization in 1938, playing third base and batting .290 in 60 games for Cedar Rapids of the Three-I League. Called up to the major leagues in September, he went 0 for 1 with a walk in a game against Detroit.

Lou moved to shortstop for the 1939 season, most of which he spent with Buffalo of the International League. There he hit .331 with 17 homers and 57 runs batted in to go along with his 32 doubles, 7 triples, and 88 runs scored before joining the parent club for the final third of the season. He didn't fare as well at the major league level that year, batting .258 with 19 RBI in 53 games.

But in 1940, Good Kid showed the Indians and the rest of the American League that he was a *great* kid. On a team that boasted the likes of Bob Feller (who pitched an opening-day no-hitter against the Chicago White Sox), slugging first baseman Hal Trosky, and another rising star—third baseman Ken Keltner—Boudreau nearly stole the headlines by hitting .295 with 101 RBI, 46 doubles, 10 triples, and 9 home runs; he scored 97 runs and led AL shortstops in fielding percentage, assists, and double plays.

Lou's run production and batting average didn't reach the same heights the following year, but his value to the Indians as an offensive weapon, a defensive star, and a team leader was obvious, and club officials named him player-manager for the 1942 season. He held this dual job through the 1950 season, when he was released. Lou finished his 15-year big-league career playing for the Boston Red Sox in 1951 and 1952.

Lou Boudreau was one Rookie of the Year who fulfilled the promise that he showed early in his career. He hit .295 lifetime and led the American League in doubles three times and batting average once. He led AL shortstops in fielding percentage eight times, double plays five times, and putouts four times.

The BBWAA named him the AL Most Valuable Player for 1948, the same season in which his bat, glove, and leadership were crucial to the Indians' first pennant since 1920. Not only did Boudreau log personal bests of .355, 18 homers, and 106 RBI, but he cracked two of his homers in an 8–3 victory over the Boston Red Sox in a one-game playoff that decided the 1948 AL Championship. The Indians beat the Boston Braves in the World Series, four games to two. Lou was flawless afield, and four of his six Series hits were doubles.

He later managed the Red Sox, the Kansas City Athletics, and the Cubs. Lou was elected to the Hall of Fame in 1970.

PETE REISER—1941

Pete Reiser during his rookie campaign.

When talk turns to the rookie season of the Brooklyn Dodgers' Pete Reiser, irony comes to mind.

Irony because "Pistol Pete" was going to be a star not for the Dodgers but for the St. Louis Cardinals—the team that had nurtured him in its farm system before baseball's commissioner, Judge Kenesaw Mountain Landis, declared Reiser and ninety other Cardinal farmhands "free agents" as a means of breaking the Cardinals' stranglehold on the country's minor leagues.

Irony because it was in a game *against* the Cardinals that the speedy outfielder smashed into the concrete wall at Sportsman's Park in St. Louis as he chased down a fly ball.

Before hitting the wall in July, the twenty-two-year-old Reiser was getting hits off NL hurlers at a rate of .390. And although his average plummeted to just above .310 at one point, Pete sufficiently regrouped to close out his rookie campaign on a high note: a league-leading .343 batting average, as well as league-leading totals in runs scored (117), triples (17), doubles (39), and slugging percentage (.558). Certainly as an acknowledgment of Pete's talent, and perhaps a little for his willingness to play despite recurring dizziness and severe headaches, the Chicago chapter of the BBWAA voted him baseball's Rookie of the Year for 1941.

Pete also put up solid numbers in 1942. In only 125 games, he hit .310 with 64 RBI and 33 doubles while scoring 89 runs. His 20 steals led the league. These numbers brought to an end the discussion of whether his head injuries from the previous season—although serious enough to cause recurring headaches and other physical ailments over the years—would end his career. It seemed he would be a top player in the National League for many years to come.

If not for World War II, this would have been the case. As was true of so many other people in the 1930s and 1940s, Pete's career (and his life) was temporarily interrupted by the Second World War—he served in the U.S. armed forces from 1943 through 1945. Rejoining the Dodgers for the 1946 season, he hit a respectable .277 with 73 RBI and 21 doubles. He also led the NL in stolen bases, with 34; seven of those steals were of home, still the major league season record he shares with Rod Carew of the Minnesota Twins. Also on Pete's ledger for 1946 was a broken ankle, which caused him to miss more than thirty games and kept him out of the lineup when the Dodgers faced the Cardinals in a best-of-three playoff series to decide the NL pennant. The Cards took the first two games from the Dodgers to earn the right to go to the World Series.

In the 1947 season, Reiser upped his batting average to .309, but saw his run production and extra-base hits drop off in part-time play. He also suffered a concussion that limited his playing time to 110 games.

Pete played sparingly for Brooklyn in 1948 before winding down his ten-year big-league career with the Braves, the Pittsburgh Pirates, and the Indians. He later coached.

JOHNNY BEAZLEY—1942

Johnny Beazley was just slightly overshadowed by teammate Mort Cooper during the 1942 regular season as the duo helped pitch the St. Louis Cardinals to the NL Championship and into the World Series.

The more experienced Cooper had a lower earned-run average than Beazley (1.77 to 2.13) and he was one victory better than his mound mate (22 to 21). The veteran completed 63 percent of the games he started; Beazley finished only 57 percent. Still, Beazley's numbers were good enough to earn him baseball's Rookie of the Year Award for 1942.

And in that year's World Series, it was the twenty-four-year-old youngster who represented the Cardinals on the mound as they faced the New York Yankees, which starred slugger Joe DiMaggio and pitchers Ernie Bonham, Spud Chandler, Red Ruffing, Atley Donald, and Hank Borowy. Beazley finished and won both games he started—including the Series-clinching Game Five—and basked in the glory that comes with securing a World Championship for a team and its fans.

But winning a World Series pales next to winning a war, and Beazley spent the next three years—prime years in the life of a young ballplayer—in the U.S. Army Air Corps.

When he returned to baseball and the Cardinals after World War II, Beazley quickly found that the arm injury he had suffered in the service spelled the end of his big-league career. He went 7–5 with a 4.46 ERA for the Cardinals in 1946 and pitched one inning of relief in a World Series that will forever be remembered for Enos Slaughter's mad dash from second to home in the eighth inning of Game Seven, the run that would eventually give the Cardinals another World Series trophy.

Johnny pitched sparingly for the Boston Braves from 1947 to 1949 before hanging up his spikes.

Cardinal great and Hall of Famer Stan Musial once said of Beazley that had he not injured his pitching arm in the war, he could have been one of the NL's best righties of that era.

Johnny Beazley in his first year with the Cardinals.

BILLY JOHNSON—1943

Almost any large city will have living in it a large number of men named William Johnson. But in New York City in 1943, one particular William Johnson became more prominent than his same-named fellow New Yorkers.

Billy "Bull" Johnson was a five-foot-ten-inch, 180-pound rookie when he took the field as the Yankees' third baseman. Defensively, he proved to be a major asset to the Yanks over the course of the season. Offensively, his five home runs that season were unimpressive. (But then, so were the home run totals of most other players in 1943—only four players in all of Major League Baseball hit more than 20 that year.)

But what Billy *did* do was drive in runs. That's how teams win ball games, and that's how the Yankees won their third straight AL crown. His 94 RBI put him third behind teammate Nick Etten (107) and the Detroit Tigers' Rudy York (118). Billy also hit .280 with 24 doubles.

For his efforts, the man with a common name was named baseball's Rookie of the Year for 1943. But even this wasn't enough for Johnson. There was still the matter of exacting revenge on the Cardinals, who had beaten the Yanks in the World Series the year before.

In the 1943 tilt, Billy led all batters with 6 hits and was second among all starters with a .300 average. In Game Three, he smacked a 3-run triple into the left-center-field gap that gave the Yankees the lead for good; moved them ahead in the Series, two games to one; and helped dash the hopes of Cardinal fans that their team might repeat as world champs.

Like most other ballplayers of this era, Johnson served his country during World War II. In missing the 1944 and 1945 baseball seasons, he may have lost some of his timing at the plate. Still, in 85 games he hit .260 with 35 RBI for the 1946 season. But Billy was back in top form in 1947 and 1948, batting .285 and .294, respectively, for those two seasons. Recalling how much he enjoyed hitting that game-winning triple in the 1943 Series, Johnson hit *three* triples in the 1947 Series as the Yanks prevailed over their archrivals, the Dodgers, in a seven-game battle that featured *that* year's Rookie of the Year, Jackie Robinson. Billy closed out his career with the Cardinals in the early 1950s.

Billy Johnson takes some batting practice cuts before Game Four of the 1943 World Series.

Did You Know?

The New York Yankees' Billy Johnson, who won the 1943 Rookie of the Year Award, still holds the record for highest fielding percentage by a rookie third baseman. He set this record by fielding at a .966 clip over the course of 155 games. Chris Sabo of the Cincinnati Reds, the 1988 NL Rookie of the Year, tied that record, but did so over 137 games. (Sabo also played two games at shortstop.) Another Yankee, Gil McDougald, fielded at a .968 clip during the 1951 season, but Gil played 55 games at second base and 82 at third base.

BILL VOISELLE—1944

The New York Giants finished fifth in the NL standings in 1944—38 games behind the pennant-winning Cardinals. The Giants had the second-highest team ERA in the league, and none of the position players led in any major offensive category. The Giants weren't awful; they just weren't much fun to watch, and Giants fans had little to cheer about.

There were bright spots, however. Popular veteran Mel Ott socked 26 dingers on his way to plating 82 runs, former Cardinal Joe Medwick hit .337, and thirty-six-year-old first baseman Phil Weintraub hit .316 and legged out 9 triples.

But the brightest spot on the squad held the No. 1 spot in the rotation: rookie pitcher Bill Voiselle. The native South Carolinian won 21 games, good for a third-place tie with the Pirates' Rip Sewell. Voiselle, a twenty-five-year-old workhorse, led the league in games started (41), innings pitched (313), and strikeouts (161). His ERA was a decent 3.02, good for fourth-best among NL hurlers with at least 250 innings pitched. These numbers earned Bill the Rookie of the Year Award for 1944.

Usually playing for mediocre teams throughout his nine-year major league career, Voiselle never matched the success of his rookie season.

As a member of the 1948 NL Champion Braves, Bill was pitted against the Indians' Bob Lemon, who, with relief help from Gene Bearden, bested Voiselle and the Braves 4–3 in the sixth and final game of the World Series.

For his career, Voiselle went 74–84 with a 3.83 ERA. He started nearly 80 percent of the games in which he appeared.

Perhaps the most interesting number associated with Voiselle is 96. That was his uniform number after he was traded to the Braves in 1947, as well as the name of his hometown: Ninety Six, South Carolina.

Bill Voiselle, pictured here in his rookie season with the New York Giants, got to the World Series in 1948 as a member of the Boston Braves.

DAVE FERRISS—1945

Red Sox pitching ace Dave Ferriss is one of about a dozen men to have pitched a shutout in each of their first two major league games. Ferriss accomplished this feat in 1945 by beating the Philadelphia Athletics 2–0 on April 29 and the Yankees 5–0 on May 6. He was twenty-three at the time.

If *that* didn't sound the wake-up call for AL batters that a tough new kid was waiting for them, nothing did. As it turned out, Ferriss went on to accumulate five shutouts that year as he compiled a 21–10 mark with a 2.96 ERA. He completed 26 of his 31 starts and also saved two games as a spot reliever.

There was no one "knock" against Dave—more like a lot of knocks, as in base knocks. He gave up 263 hits in 265 innings that first year and 274 hits in 274 innings in 1946.

The difference between Dave's rookie season, when the Red Sox finished a dismal seventh in an eight-team league, and 1946, when the Red Sox won the AL Championship and went to the World Series, is that the 1946 squad had most of its top players back in a baseball uniform after they had worn military issue while serving in World War II. Ted Williams, Dom DiMaggio, Johnny Pesky, Bobby Doerr, and Dave's fellow starting pitchers Tex Hughson, Mickey Harris, and Joe Dobson were just some of the Red Sox players who had returned from the war.

Ferriss was named baseball's Rookie of the Year for 1945. This was a well-deserved honor for a man who was the only pitcher on his team to win in double figures that year.

Dave didn't stop being the team's ace when the 1946 season arrived. In fact, he posted a much better record (25–6) and strikeout-to-walk total (106 to 71) than even he might have hoped for. Although the Red Sox lost the 1946 Series to the Cardinals, Ferriss pitched a six-hit shutout in Game Three.

Dave went 12–11 in 1947 and 7–3 in 1948. He appeared in only a few games over the next two years, and by 1951 his career was over.

Dave Ferriss in 1945. A sore arm prematurely ended his career five years later.

EDDIE WAITKUS—1946

Eddie Waitkus at spring training in 1947, just before the opening of his sophomore season.

Bernard Malamud's 1952 novel, *The Natural*, and Robert Redford's 1984 film of the same title are not about Eddie Waitkus, but they do echo an incident in the life and career of the former first baseman following his four-year hitch with Uncle Sam in World War II.

Waitkus debuted with the Cubs in April 1941 as a twenty-one-year-old rookie. He played in only 12 games, and his batting average barely topped his weight (170). He didn't see much action in the field, either.

Eddie served his country in World War II, and as a result did not play baseball from 1942 through 1945. When he returned to baseball in 1946, his batting stroke had greatly improved. Eddie hit .304 for the Cubs that year, knocking in 55 runs and scoring another 50 in 113 games. He walked just 23 times, but struck out only 14 times. Simply stated, Waitkus had a good eye at the plate and was good at putting the ball into play. He was also one of the top-fielding first basemen in the National League, committing only four errors. He was named Rookie of the Year for 1946.

He hit close to .300 during the next two seasons, before the Cubs traded him to the Philadelphia Phillies, and in 1949 he was off to a great start. He was a .300 hitter and in double figures in RBI and doubles through the first third of the season. Even better, he was playing for a team that was in the pennant chase. He had his health and he hadn't turned thirty yet. Life for Eddie Waitkus was good.

But on June 14, a mentally disturbed female fan—who had checked into the same Chicago hotel where the visiting Phillies were staying—tricked Eddie into coming to her room. There, the nineteen-year-old woman pulled out a .22-caliber rifle and shot Eddie in the chest. Barely missing his heart, the bullet lodged near his spine and caused his right lung to collapse. At the hospital, Waitkus received blood transfusions and oxygen, and the doctors and nurses saved his life. The would-be killer was later sent to a mental institution.

Eddie Waitkus returned to baseball in 1950, helping the Phillies win the NL pennant while he earned the second major award of his career: Comeback Player of the Year. He continued to play through the 1955 season. Eddie hit .285 in an eleven-year career that was interrupted once each by a world and a fan gone mad.

JACKIE ROBINSON—1947

The great Jackie Robinson at the plate, about to uncoil as the pitch zooms plateward.

Jackie Robinson's best year at the plate was 1949, when he won the Most Valuable Player Award after leading the National League in batting with a .342 average. He knocked in 124 runs, scored 122, and hit 16 homers, 12 triples, and 38 doubles. He also stole 37 bases, the most in either league that year. Without him, the Brooklyn Dodgers would have coughed up the pennant to the hard-charging St. Louis Cardinals.

But it was his rookie season—1947—for which most people remember Jackie. He wasn't the first black man to wear a major league uniform, but he was the first to prop open the door that baseball had kept shut for so long. It was his combination of pride, savvy, athletic ability, and burning desire to win that turned not just the world of baseball, but the world at large, into a better place.

When the dust had settled after that historic and fascinating season, Robinson had accumulated a .297 batting average, 125 runs scored, 48 RBI, 12 homers, 5 triples, and 31 doubles. He paced the league in steals with 29.

The national organization of the Baseball Writers' Association of America had by this time wrested from its Chicago chapter the job of awarding Rookie of the Year honors to baseball's best young talent. The voting for the 1947 honoree was close, but in the end Jackie beat out the fine young right-hander for the New York Giants, Larry Jansen, who went 21–5 that year with a 3.16 ERA.

Robinson was twenty-eight when he broke in with the Dodgers in 1947, the oldest of any Rookie of the Year to that point. But Jackie's debut season was no fluke, as the statistics of his 10-year career—all with Brooklyn—show: a .311 batting average, 734 RBI, 947 runs scored, 137 home runs, 54 triples, 273 doubles, and 197 stolen bases, including 19 of home.

At the 1987 Hall of Fame induction ceremonies in Cooperstown, New York, Commissioner Peter Ueberroth proclaimed that the Rookie of the Year Award would now officially be known as the Jackie Robinson Award.

ALVIN DARK—1948

Alvin Dark in his first year with the Braves. Years later, he became a successful manager.

Alvin Dark could do it all. Over the course of his twenty-seven-year career in baseball, the gifted Oklahoman played every outfield and infield position, pitched (albeit in just one game, in 1953, and he was mercifully removed after one inning), coached, and managed.

He wasn't a base stealer, but he was swift, and doubles were his specialty. (With the exception of being brought up for his proverbial "cup of coffee" in 1946 when he hit 3 in 13 at-bats, Dark was always in double figures in doubles, and he led the National League in that department in 1951.) And his defensive abilities—notably at shortstop, his best position—were solid if not flashy. Dark and second baseman Eddie Stanky gave the Giants of the early 1950s one of the better double-play duos of the period.

But it was as a rookie with the Boston Braves in 1948 that Dark established himself as a big-league talent who was here to stay. He batted .322 (the best single-season average of his career) with 39 doubles, 85 runs scored, and 175 hits. That kind of inaugural season assured him of the Rookie of the Year honors for 1948.

Indeed, he was instrumental in the Braves' pennant drive, which was immortalized by the saying, "Spahn and Sain and two days of rain," a nod to the pitching heroics of Warren and Johnny, respectively, who combined for nearly 40 of the Braves' 91 wins that year.

Alvin struggled in the 1948 World Series against the Cleveland Indians, mustering only a .167 batting average and committing three errors. But he made up for this poor showing a few years later as a member of the Giants, hitting for a .417 average with no errors in the 1951 Series and .412 with 1 error but a Series-leading 12 assists in the 1954 October Classic.

Dark stayed in the game after his playing days were over. His greatest successes as a manager came in 1962, when he guided the San Francisco Giants to first place and a World Series appearance, and in 1974, when he guided the Oakland A's to a World Championship.

Alvin's lifetime stats as a player include a .289 batting average, 757 RBI, 1,064 runs scored, and nearly 2,100 hits.

Winners by Position

Outfielders and pitchers have dominated Rookie of the Year voting since the award was created in 1940. That's no surprise, considering there are more players at those two positions than at any other, and that there is also more turnover at those two positions, from one year to the next, than at any other. Here, then, is the breakdown, by position, of Rookie of the Year winners from 1940 through 1995:

Outfielders: 31
Pitchers: 27
First basemen: 13
Shortstops: 11
Second basemen: 8
Third basemen: 8
Catchers: 7

Note: In their rookie seasons, several players—notably Gil McDougald (AL 1951), Tony Kubek (AL 1957), Tom Tresh (AL 1962), and Cal Ripken Jr. (AL 1982)—played multiple positions. For this list, such players are grouped according to the position at which they played the most games in their rookie seasons.

ROY SIEVERS—AL 1949

"I think 1957, when I was with the [Washington] Senators, was my greatest year in baseball," Roy Sievers once told an interviewer. "That was the year I beat out Mickey Mantle and Ted Williams for the home-run crown and also led the league in RBI while hitting over .300.

"But my rookie year, in 1949, was my best with the [St. Louis] Browns, no question about it."

Apparently, the BBWAA thought so, too—its membership named Sievers the AL Rookie of the Year for 1949, the first year in which *two* players—one from each league—were accorded this honor. Roy, then twenty-two, had knocked in 91 runs, scored 84, hit 16 home runs and 28 doubles, and batted .306 that year. All that for a seventh-place team in an eight-team league.

In fact, it was Roy's misfortune to play mostly for second-division teams throughout his seventeen-year career. He was once on a third-place team, twice on a fourth-place team, and once on a sixth-place team. He would have been on a second-place team, the 1964 Philadelphia Phillies, but the Phillies traded him to the ninth-place Senators over in the American League before the season was over, sparing Roy from being part of the haunted 1964 Phils, who blew a six-and-a-half-game lead—and the NL pennant in the process—with just two weeks remaining in the regular season.

Despite serving mostly on teams basking in the quiet that is seventh and eighth place, Sievers fashioned a superb baseball ledger for himself.

Roy's rookie campaign gave the fans a glimpse of what this slugger could do with a bat, although he had several off-years before hitting his stride in the mid-1950s. There were seasons of 20, 30, even 40 home runs or more; RBI totals in the 80s, 90s, and 100s; and batting averages as high as .295 and .301—serious numbers put up by an easygoing guy with a passion for playing the game. And for a power hitter, Roy had a good eye at the plate. Only in his last few full seasons did his strikeouts far surpass his walks.

The 1949 AL Rookie of the Year holds another distinction: actual game footage of him as a Senator in the 1950s was used in the 1958 movie musical *Damn Yankees.*

"I think the filmmakers used clips of me hitting home runs off Whitey Ford," Roy said. "What happens is that you see me hitting the ball, and when they cut the scene, you see Tab Hunter runnin' the bases."

Roy Sievers at Sportsman's Park, St. Louis, on May 15, 1949.

DON NEWCOMBE—NL 1949

Pitching ace Don Newcombe didn't need singer-songwriter Terry Cashman to immortalize him in the song "Willie, Mickey and the Duke (Talkin' Baseball)" because "Newk" did just fine on his own.

The New Jersey native broke in with the Dodgers in 1949 and proceeded to mow down NL hitters. He completed 19 of his 31 starts en route to a 17–8 record with a 3.17 ERA and five shutouts, including a 3–0 blanking of the Cincinnati Reds in May. That little gem was the first start in Newk's ten-year career in the majors. He also pitched 244 innings and compiled twice as many strikeouts as walks. For all that, Don was runaway winner of the 1949 NL Rookie of the Year Award.

He won 19 games in his sophomore season, and established himself as a key player in the Dodgers' glory years of the 1950s. Newcombe went 20–9 in 1951, 20–5 in 1955, and 27–7 in 1956. Also in 1956, he not only received the first Cy Young Award for being the best pitcher in the major leagues, but also was awarded NL Most Valuable Player honors.

Although he never won a World Series game (he had 4 losses and 1 no-decision in 5 starts over three World Series), Don Newcombe was always considered one of the more dependable pitchers of his era. Newk loved to hit, too. He had a .271 lifetime batting average complemented by 15 homers and 108 RBI. Seven of his dingers came in 1955.

Don Newcombe winding up for a pitch.

C H A P T E R   T W O

THE 1950s

WALT DROPO—AL 1950

Had Whitey Ford pitched a full season for the New York Yankees in 1950—he debuted in July and went 9–1 with a 2.81 ERA and 1 save—he may have won AL Rookie of the Year honors. But he didn't, and so Walt Dropo of the Boston Red Sox was a fairly easy choice for the BBWAA.

The numbers Dropo put up were, to use teammate Bobby Doerr's term, "truly gaudy." In just 136 games, the slugging first baseman hit .322 with 34 home runs, 8 triples, and 28 doubles. He scored 101 runs, and his 144 runs batted in—which tied him for the league lead that year—are one shy of the all-time major league record for rookie hitters. (The man who holds that distinction was another Red Sox slugger—Ted Williams, who knocked in 145 in 1939.)

Walt never came close to having another season like his first, but he put together a good career that spanned thirteen years and five clubs. In various seasons, he hit as many as 29 home runs, knocked in as many as 97 runs, and batted in the low .280s. Throughout the 1950s, he was a reliable first baseman and one of the more feared hitters in the middle of the lineup.

Walt Dropo awaiting a pitch.

Sam Jethroe starred for the Braves in the early 1950s.

SAM JETHROE—NL 1950

Like Jackie Robinson before him, Sam Jethroe had played in the Negro Leagues, played for the Montreal Royals in the International League, and was twenty-eight years old when he finally got to the big leagues.

But unlike the pathfinder, Sam was a true star of all-black baseball; from 1944 through 1946, he led the Negro National League in batting average and stolen bases, and he was a fan favorite wherever he went.

At Triple-A Montreal in 1949, Sam's .326 batting average and his league-leading 89 stolen bases, 19 triples, and 154 runs scored easily made him a household name in all of baseball, not just among Negro League aficionados.

Feeling, perhaps, that it had an abundance of black talent and could afford to let go of some of its minority players for much-needed cash, the Dodgers organization sold Jethroe to the Boston Braves. He debuted with the Braves in April 1950 and quickly established himself as a big-league talent. The Braves' first black player, Jethroe was a solid hitter and a graceful outfielder.

At the end of the exciting 1950 season, Sam had accumulated a .273 batting average, 18 homers, 58 RBI, 100 runs scored, 8 triples, 28 doubles, and a league-leading 35 stolen bases in 141 games. He didn't do as well on defense, though; he had 12 outfield errors, the worst in the league. However, Sam also had 17 assists (second in the league) and 6 double plays. Ladies and gentlemen, meet the 1950 NL Rookie of the Year.

Sam played in the majors for just three more years after that superb rookie season. In 1951 he improved in nearly all offensive categories, and again led the majors in steals, with 35 (he was caught only five times).

Although his batting average dropped to .232 in 1952, he still managed to hit 13 home runs with 58 RBI to go with his 28 stolen bases. He did not play for Boston in 1953, and at Christmastime he was traded to the Pittsburgh Pirates, for whom he appeared in just two games in 1954. The "Jet," as Jethroe was called, went on to star for Toronto of the International League through the 1958 season before ending his career.

GIL McDOUGALD—AL 1951

Rookie sensation Gil McDougald was in the right place (the Yankees organization) at the right time (1951) when he started his baseball career. He was a big part of why the pinstripers were in the middle of their record-setting five consecutive World Championship seasons.

The native San Franciscan divided his time between third base and second base that year, and played well for the Yanks in 131 games. But it was his bat, not his glove, that impressed people the most. McDougald's 63 RBI were fueled by a .306 batting average that included 23 doubles and 14 home runs. He also stole 14 bases and scored 72 runs.

Those numbers were good enough to win McDougald AL Rookie of the Year honors. (His closest competitor for the award was Minnie Minoso, who put on quite a show of his own in 1951 as a member of both the Cleveland Indians and the Chicago White Sox: a .326 average, league-leading totals in triples [14] and stolen bases [31], 76 RBI, and 112 runs scored.)

Gil's ten years in the big leagues, all spent with the Yankees, were a tribute to his consistency. He never put up Most Valuable Player numbers, but he always contributed to the Yankees' run production. He was almost always in the middle of a Yankees rally, and he helped the club to eight World Series. As a rookie in his first World Series, Gil knocked in 7 runs. In the 1952 Series, he had 3 RBI. In both the 1953 and 1958 tilts, he had 4.

Lifetime, McDougald hit .276 with 112 home runs and 576 RBI.

In 1957 (one of his better offensive campaigns), Gil lined 9 triples, which tied him with teammates Hank Bauer and Harry Simpson for the AL lead.

Gil McDougald swatted ten homers in eight World Series.

WILLIE MAYS—NL 1951

At a baseball card convention held a few years before Leo Durocher died, he was signing autographs at the same table as Willie Mays. Talking with an interviewer, "The Lip" rattled off his oft-quoted lines about Mays being the "greatest player I ever saw" and about his former charge's ability to "do it all—hit, hit with power, run, field, and throw."

But in a truly warm, reflective moment, Leo paused, looked at the 1954 World Championship ring that he always wore, and quietly said: "Willie helped me get this."

Mays was indeed a key reason why the New York Giants were baseball's best team in 1954. He topped the National League in batting average, slugging percentage, and triples, and he poled 41 homers on his way to 110 RBI and the NL's MVP Award.

His numbers in 1951, his first season in the big leagues, were not as eye-popping, but they were good enough to secure him the NL Rookie of the Year Award. The young Giant hit .274 with 68 RBI, 20 home runs, and 22 doubles. In the field, he played well if not spectacularly. He would in time become one of the game's premier outfielders, though, and his running, over-the-shoulder catch of Vic Wertz's booming fly ball in the 1954 World Series still ranks as one of baseball's greatest defensive plays.

His career totals, including 660 homers, more than 1,900 RBI, and a .302 batting average, aren't all that bad, considering he began his rookie season mired in a horrible slump.

Mays led the NL in home runs four times, triples twice (plus another year in which he tied for league lead), and runs scored twice. He closed out his career with the New York Mets in the early 1970s.

It was said of his superb fielding: "His glove is where triples go to die."

Willie Mays stretches for a fly ball in 1951.

HARRY BYRD—AL 1952

Perhaps it was his potential, as much as his initial impact on the league, that the BBWAA was looking at when it selected pitcher Harry Byrd of the Philadelphia Athletics as its AL Rookie of the Year for 1952.

In retrospect his numbers don't seem impressive—a .500 record with a 3.31 ERA and 244 hits allowed in 228 innings—but the strapping righty from Darlington, South Carolina, had the stuff to win 15 games (three of them shutouts) and save 2 others in his rookie season, and that was enough to convince the BBWAA's members to vote for him over two rookie catchers, Clint Courtney and Sammy White, who would each play for eleven years before retiring.

Byrd was a workhorse for the A's. In 1953 he led the American League in games started (37). He also led the league in losses (20), as the combination of his control problems (he walked almost as many batters as he struck out, and he gave up 279 hits in 237 innings) and pitching for a seventh-place team in an eight-team league proved deadly.

He fared a little better the following season as a member of the Yankees, when he went 9–7 with a 2.99 ERA. Unfortunately, that was the *only* year between 1949 and 1958 that the Yanks *didn't* win the AL flag, so Byrd was never part of a championship club.

Byrd played briefly for the Baltimore Orioles and White Sox before closing out his seven-year career with the Detroit Tigers, where he was used almost exclusively in relief. In his last season, 1957, Harry went 4–3 with five saves and a 3.36 ERA, a pretty good way to cap off an award-winning career.

Harry Byrd strikes an action pose in 1953, his second year in the major leagues.

Joe Black on the mound in 1953, the season after he was named NL Rookie of the Year.

JOE BLACK—NL 1952

What was it about twenty-eight-year-old former Negro Leaguers? Joe Black became the third such player, following Jackie Robinson and Sam Jethroe, to win the Rookie of the Year Award.

Joe wasn't on the Brooklyn Dodgers' spring roster for 1952, but those responsible for correcting that situation before the season got underway must have looked like geniuses in October, when the Dodgers faced the Yankees in the World Series.

Black was the key to the Dodgers' winning their third pennant in six years. His 15 saves matched his 15 wins—against only 4 losses—and his sterling 2.15 ERA established him as a pitcher to be reckoned with.

Dodgers manager Charlie Dressen was so confident in Joe's pitching that he called on Joe to start Game One of the Series. Despite having started only two games during the regular season, Joe pitched a complete game and won 4–2 against a Yankee lineup that included Mickey Mantle, Gil McDougald, Yogi Berra, Joe Collins, Gene Woodling, and Hank Bauer.

However, Black was the 2–0 tough-luck loser in Game Four, even though he allowed only 3 hits and 1 run in 7 innings. He also lost the decisive Game Seven on a Mantle homer in the sixth that put the Yanks ahead for good.

Joe never quite had the success in subsequent years that he had in his glorious rookie campaign, and he was out of the majors by the end of the 1957 season.

In his six seasons in the big leagues—spent mostly as a reliever—Joe went 30–12 for a .714 winning percentage.

HARVEY KUENN—AL 1953

Younger fans who watched manager Harvey Kuenn guide the Milwaukee Brewers to the 1982 AL Championship may not have been aware of Kuenn's previous life as a superb contact hitter.

But between 1953—when he won AL Rookie of the Year honors—and 1959, his last year with Detroit but only the halfway point in his playing career, Kuenn led the league in hits three times (and tied for the lead a fourth time), doubles three times, and batting average once.

As a speedy glove man, mostly at shortstop and in the outfield, Kuenn was able to get to batted balls that lesser mortals would not have reached, but that also meant he was subject to making a greater number of errors. Indeed, his errors were in double figures for five straight years with the Tigers, but during that time he also led the league twice in total putouts, once in assists, and once in fielding percentage.

His lifetime batting average was .303 over all or part of fifteen seasons, and his 356 doubles and 951 runs scored attest that Harvey Kuenn was one of those players who hustle down the line on every play.

Kuenn's statistics for his rookie season—a .308 batting average, a league-leading 209 total hits, 94 runs scored, 33 doubles, and, on defense, a league-leading 308 putouts at shortstop—made him the clear favorite in the eyes of the BBWAA membership.

Harvey was an integral part of the 1962 San Francisco Giants' successful pennant drive, hitting .304 and knocking in 68 runs. That year, he was one-third of an all-.300-hitting outfield (Willie Mays also hit .304 and Felipe Alou hit .316).

Following his career as a player, Kuenn served as a Brewers coach for a dozen years and as their manager for two.

Tiger rookie shortstop Harvey Kuenn fires the ball to first after beating 1951 AL Rookie of the Year Gil McDougald to the second-base bag.

JIM GILLIAM—NL 1953

The Dodgers organization and Branch Rickey had parted company by 1951, but the former president and general manager's policy of mining the Negro Leagues for fresh talent was still in place and still crucial to the club's continuing dominance of the National League.

Jim "Junior" Gilliam was a superb second baseman culled from the Baltimore Elite Giants. Jim had a great eye at the plate and a pair of legs that turned his singles into doubles and his doubles into triples. A versatile defensive player, he also played third base, first base, and outfield during his fourteen-year career, all with the Brooklyn/Los Angeles Dodgers. He later also coached for the Dodgers from 1965 to 1978.

Gilliam burst onto the big-league scene in 1953 with 17 triples—tops in the majors that year. He also hit 31 doubles and 6 home runs to go with his .278 batting average, 125 runs scored, and 63 RBI. He drew 100 walks and struck out just 38 times. About the only place where the opposition got the better of him was on the basepaths, where he was thrown out in 40 percent of his attempted steals.

The BBWAA voted Gilliam the NL Rookie of the Year for 1953. He was the fourth former Negro Leaguer turned Dodger in seven years to win Rookie of the Year honors.

Jim Gilliam played in seven World Series for the Dodgers, and, offensively anyway, his first series, in 1953, was his best. Nevertheless, he will always be remembered for his outstanding diving stop of Zoilo Versalles' hard-hit ball down the third-base line in Game Seven of the 1965 World Series against the Minnesota Twins. Jim stepped onto third to force Frank Quilici for the second out in what was shaping up to be a Twins rally in the fifth inning. The Twins failed to score and the Dodgers held on for the 2–0 win and the Series victory.

The Dodgers had a real find in Jim Gilliam, shown here during his rookie season.

BOB GRIM—AL 1954

Yankee pitcher Bob Grim leans back into a pitch during a 1957 practice.

Bob Grim never matched the success of his rookie season, but in his first year as a member of the Yankees 1950s juggernaut, he was outstanding.

Grim went 20–6 with a 3.26 ERA while allowing only 175 hits in 199 innings. He struck out 108 batters and walked 85. The BBWAA named him the AL Rookie of the Year for 1954.

Too bad for Grim and his fellow pinstripers, who notched 103 victories that season, that they were in the same league as the the Indians. All Cleveland did was win an AL-record 111 games—and the pennant.

Eight of Bob's 20 wins in 1954 came in relief—a harbinger, perhaps, of things to come. By 1957, the Yankees were using him exclusively out of the bullpen. His 19 saves that year led the league's relievers, as did his 12 wins and 8 losses.

The native New Yorker was used mostly as a starter by the 1958 Kansas City Athletics, who brought him aboard in a mid-June trade. Later, however, as Grim finished out the string with Cleveland, Cincinnati, St. Louis, and Kansas City for a second tour, he returned to his familiar role as reliever.

WALLY MOON—NL 1954

The term "moon shot," coined during the formative stages of America's space program in the late 1950s, is baseball lingo for a long home run. Wally Moon, who knew more about launching home runs than about launching artificial earth satellites, forged a twelve-year career with the St. Louis Cardinals and the Los Angeles Dodgers that featured several Moon shots.

In fact, Wally hit a home run in his first big-league appearance, on April 13, 1954. It was the first of 12 that he hit that year to go with his 76 RBI, 106 runs scored, .304 batting average, 29 doubles, and 9 triples.

The Cardinal was swiftly named the NL Rookie of the Year for 1954, the first Redbird to take home rookie honors since Johnny Beazley in 1942. Moon was in some excellent rookie company in 1954. Also vying for top-rookie honors that year were pitcher Gene Conley (14–9, with a 2.96 ERA) and future Hall of Famers Ernie Banks and Henry Aaron.

Moon wasn't flashy; he just got the job done. He hit better than .300 for a season three times (he hit in the high .290s four times), and was in double figures in homers seven times, including a career-high 24 in 1957.

In 1959, his first year as a Dodger, Moon tied teammate Charlie Neal for the major-league lead in triples, with 11. He also hit .302 with 19 moon shots, 26 doubles, and 74 RBI. He also scored 93 runs, the second-highest total on the team. Moon was essential to the Dodgers' successful pennant drive. As a capper to this incredible season, he hit a two-run homer in Game Six of the World Series against the "Go-Go" White Sox to help win the game and the Series.

Wally Moon slides into home plate as Dodger catcher Roy Campanella loses the ball during the Brooklyn–St. Louis game at Ebbets Field on June 27, 1954.

HERB SCORE—AL 1955

Hall of Famer Harmon Killebrew, who socked 573 home runs in his stellar major league career, said Cleveland fireballer Herb Score "threw harder than anyone I ever saw. He was amazing." This from a man who faced Sandy Koufax, Nolan Ryan, Denny McLain, and Don Drysdale in their hard-throwing prime.

Score was named the 1955 AL Rookie of the Year for his 16–10 record, 2.85 ERA, and 245 strikeouts, the most in the major leagues that year and an AL record for rookie pitchers. Sixteen of those 245 Ks came in one game, played against the Red Sox in early May.

As good as Herb was in his rookie season, he was even better the next year, when he went 20–9 with a 2.53 ERA and a whopping 263 strikeouts in 249 innings. He allowed only 162 hits, notched 5 shutouts, and pitched 16 complete games.

About a month into the 1957 season, Score had posted a 2–1 record with an ERA at 2.00, when the Yankees' Gil McDougald—1951's top AL rookie—smoked a line drive that struck Score in the right eye, crushing his nose and clouding his vision. The Indians lost him for the season. Although he eventually recovered from the terrifying blow and continued to pitch into the 1962 season, Score never regained the momentum he had going for him earlier in his career.

In 1960, Herb was traded to the White Sox, with whom he finished his career. He has been a member of the Indians' broadcasting team since his retirement after the 1962 season.

Herb Score warms up before a game.

BILL VIRDON—NL 1955

Two teams let young Bill Virdon slip away. The first was the Yankees, who signed him to a minor league contract in 1949 but traded him to St. Louis for Enos Slaughter in 1954. The second was the Cardinals, who gave up on him all too soon in 1956, when, early in the season, both he and the team were struggling.

The Pittsburgh Pirates were the recipients of the other two teams' generosity (or bad judgment). The Pirates kept Virdon for the rest of his big-league career—another ten years—and watched as he performed solidly in the outfield and at the plate. He never amassed eye-popping offensive numbers, but he was all business on the field. His hustle and his leadership qualities later served him well as a manager in both leagues during the 1970s and 1980s.

He is perhaps best remembered for his bad-hop single that struck Yankee shortstop Tony Kubek in the throat in the eighth inning of Game Seven of the 1960 World Series. That base hit helped spark a five-run rally in a seesaw battle won by the Pirates on Bill Mazeroski's ninth-inning homer.

Virdon's debut season, 1955, wowed the BBWAA membership enough to ensure his winning the Rookie of the Year Award. His numbers included a .281 batting average, 68 RBI, 17 homers, 6 triples, and 18 doubles. With that kind of promise, it seems odd that the Cardinals failed to keep him.

In a 1989 interview, Bill said he was surprised the Cardinals traded him. Noting that trades have always been a part of the game, he added: "I didn't figure on leaving St. Louis so soon, especially after my rookie season. I thought I was going to be there awhile."

Virdon went on to hit .267 for his career. He was rarely a home-run threat, but he often hit a fair number of doubles and triples (his 10 triples paced the National League in 1962). The irony of Bill's dearth of home runs is that in his final season, 1968, his only hit in 3 at-bats was a pinch-hit home run.

Bill Virdon began his lengthy career in 1955 as an outfielder for St. Louis.

LUIS APARICIO—AL 1956

Luis Aparicio was hero to many children in the 1950s and 1960s who aspired to be big-league shortstops.

"Little Looie," as he was often called, was a defensive wizard long before Ozzie Smith played his first sandlot game. Aparicio led the American League in fielding percentage eight times, assists seven times, and putouts five times. For nearly a decade, Aparicio teamed up with second baseman Nellie Fox to form one of baseball's top double-play tandems.

He stole 506 bases in his eighteen-year major league career. Maury Wills, who was Aparicio's contemporary over in the National League and the man who electrified the game with his daring on the basepaths in the early 1960s, stole 80 bases more than Aparicio in 657 fewer games. But Little Looie's 79 percent success rate in stealing bases is better than Wills' 74 percent.

Aparicio won the 1956 AL Rookie of the Year Award with a .266 batting average, 56 RBI, 69 runs scored, 21 steals, and 28 extra-base hits for the White Sox. For nine consecutive years—beginning with his 1956 rookie season and ending in 1964, by which time he was playing for the Orioles—Little Looie led the American League in stolen bases.

He was named to the Hall of Fame in 1984.

Also a great glove man, Luis Aparicio helped revive the art of stealing bases. He led the American League in steals for nine consecutive years, beginning with his rookie season.

FRANK ROBINSON—NL 1956

Late in his career, Frank Robinson was qoated as saying, "Close only counts in horseshoes and grenades."

A first baseman who used to play against Frank Robinson once said of the powerfully built slugger that he "scared the hell out of me whenever he hit the ball in the infield and the play was at first. It wasn't that he was terribly fast, but once he hit his stride I could hear his cleats kick up all those pebbles and dirt as he raced to the bag. He sounded like a horse, comin' down to first. I was sure that if we ever collided that he'd knock my head off."

It wasn't that Robinson was mean-spirited. It's just that he played the game of baseball full-out, and both he and the teams he played on had a lot of success because of it.

"Robbie" played the lion's share of his career with two clubs: the Baltimore Orioles and the Cincinnati Reds. As a big bopper for thé Orioles, he won baseball's Triple Crown and a Most Valuable Player trophy in 1966, and he played in four World Series over a six-year span. As an even bigger bopper for the Reds during the first ten years of his career, he hit 324 of his 586 career home runs, won his first MVP trophy, and went to a World Series.

Robinson also won the NL Rookie of the Year Award in 1956 as a member of the Reds. He belted so many balls out of the ballpark that season—38—that opposing pitchers suffered whiplash when they watched their mistakes sail out of sight. Those 38 home runs remain a rookie record, which Frank shares with Wally Berger of the 1930 Boston Braves.

In that memorable debut season, Frank also hit .290, drove in 83 runs, scored a league-leading 122 runs, and cracked 27 doubles and 6 triples. The BBWAA made him its first unanimous choice for Rookie of the Year honors.

He later proved that he had been an excellent student of the game all along. At various times in his big-league career, Robbie served as a coach, a manager, and a player-manager. He was named to the Hall of Fame in 1982.

Did You Know?

Frank Robinson, the 1956 NL Rookie of the Year, was the first black manager in both the American League (1975, with the Cleveland Indians) and the National League (1981, with the San Francisco Giants).

TONY KUBEK—AL 1957

Tony Kubek puts leather to the horsehide during spring training in 1957.

Many of today's younger baseball fans know Tony Kubek only as a broadcaster (or possibly an author), but many baby boomers can recall what a fine shortstop the Milwaukee native was for the Yankees during his nine-year career in the major leagues. (He was also quite versatile—he played the other three infield positions as well as the outfield.)

For several years, Kubek and second baseman Bobby Richardson formed one of the better double-play combos in baseball. (Together, they turned a league-leading 243 twin killings in 1961.) And Kubek was no slouch with the bat, either. He could usually be counted on for driving in about 40 or 50 runs a season, and although he never hit a lot of home runs—his 14 in 1960 were an anomaly—most years he did get a fair number of doubles and usually hit for a very respectable average.

Tony debuted with the Yankees, the only team he ever played with at the big-league level, in 1957. He hit .297 with 39 RBI and 21 doubles in 127 games as a utility player. He also scored 56 runs. The offensive numbers didn't dazzle anyone, but they—along with his versatility—were good enough to earn him the 1957 AL Rookie of the Year Award.

In that year's World Series against the Milwaukee Braves, the rookie hit .286 and cranked out 2 homers in front of the hometown fans in Game Three, but his throwing error in Game Seven kept a Braves rally alive and they went on to win the Series.

Tony and his teammates exacted revenge on the Braves in the 1958 Series, however, when the Yankees beat Milwaukee 6–2 in Game Seven to reclaim the Series title. Tony contributed a sacrifice fly to the winning cause.

In recent years, Kubek has become a top-flight and outspoken baseball analyst, and *Sixty-One,* a book he cowrote with Terry Pluto, is a fine remembrance of Roger Maris and the rest of the 1961 Yankee powerhouse.

JACK SANFORD—NL 1957

Several things impressed the BBWAA when it chose Philadelphia's Jack Sanford as the 1957 NL Rookie of the Year.

First, there was his record—19 wins and 8 losses. Second, there was his 3.08 ERA, which ranked him among the league leaders that year for pitchers who threw more than 220 total innings. Then there were his 15 complete games and 3 shutouts. And finally, there was the matter of his outstanding 188 strikeouts, tops in the majors that year.

Sanford pitched for the Phillies for two more years before being traded to the San Francisco Giants, for whom he went 24–7 in the Giants' pennant-winning season of 1962. In the World Series, he won 1 and lost 2, including the heartbreaking 1–0 loss in Game Seven, which ended when Yankee second baseman Bobby Richardson snared Willie McCovey's liner that would have scored the tying run—and perhaps the winning run, too—with two out in the bottom of the ninth.

Jack found success as a reliever as well, but that came later in his twelve-year big-league career. In 1966, when he was pitching for the California Angels, he won 12 games while losing 4 and saving 5, all in relief. He also won 1 game and lost 3 others as a starter.

Jack Sanford in action against the New York Giants in Philadelphia on April 28, 1957.

ALBIE PEARSON—AL 1958

Albie Pearson got enough playing time with the 1958 Washington Senators to hit for a .275 batting average, score 63 runs, and smack 25 doubles, all of which led to his being named the AL Rookie of the Year.

He was reduced to being a part-time player for the next two years. By the end of this period, though, the 140-pound outfielder was plying his trade in Baltimore.

But it was with the Los Angeles/California Angels that Pearson had his greatest success. He hit as high as .304 (in 1963), and his average over five full seasons was .275, the same as that for his rookie season.

Pearson had a very good eye at the plate; for several consecutive years in the early 1960s, he walked far more often than he struck out. So, with such run producers as Leon Wagner, Lee Thomas, and Ken Hunt in the Angels' lineup, Pearson scored a lot of runs, including a league high of 115 in 1962. That year he also reached career highs in doubles (29) and triples (6). A back injury limited him to only a pair of games in 1966, at which point his big-league career came to a close.

Albie Pearson strikes a baseball card pose.

Sorry, Al

Formal guidelines for determining rookie status were not established until 1957. Al Rosen, whose 37 homers led the American League in 1950, wasn't even considered for the award that year. Why? Prior to the 1950 season, he had accumulated a total of 58 big-league at-bats—too many, in the view of BBWAA voters, for Rosen to be considered a rookie. AL Rookie of the Year Walt Dropo, who that year bludgeoned opposing pitchers for 34 homers, a .322 batting average, and a league-tieing 144 RBI, had—prior to the 1950 season—accumulated 41 big-league at-bats, just 17 fewer than Rosen's 58.

ORLANDO CEPEDA—NL 1958

Orlando Cepeda before a 1958 game against the Reds at Cincinnati's Crosley Field.

Orlando Cepeda was known by the nicknames "Baby Bull" and "Cha Cha," but opposing pitchers just called him "scary."

Cepeda was a linchpin of the power-laden San Francisco Giants of the late 1950s and early to mid-1960s. From 1958, his first season in the big leagues, through 1964, when the Giants made a serious run at the NL pennant, Cepeda never hit fewer than 24 home runs, and he batted below .300 only once. In 1961, he paced the league with 46 homers, and his 142 RBI tied him with the Yankees' Roger Maris for the best in that category for both leagues.

In 1962, the year the Dodgers lost the pennant to the Giants, eight San Francisco players combined for 188 of the club's league-leading total of 204 round-trippers: Cepeda (35 home runs), Willie Mays (a big-league-high 49), Felipe Alou (25), Willie McCovey (20), Tom Haller (18), Ed Bailey (17), Jim Davenport (14), and Harvey Kuenn (10). The Giants also led in RBI (807), runs scored (878), batting average (.278), hits (1,552), and slugging percentage (.441). The Giants didn't fare as well in the World Series, though—they lost to the Yankees in seven games.

Orlando won the NL MVP Award in 1967 on his way to leading his new team, the Cardinals, to a World Championship.

But Cha Cha's debut season was among his best. He hit .312, blasted 25 home runs and a league-leading 38 doubles, knocked in 96 runs, and forged a .512 slugging percentage. For his efforts, he became the second player to be unanimously selected as Rookie of the Year.

Cepeda retired after the 1974 campaign. Over the course of his seventeen-year big-league career, he hit .297 with 379 homers and 1,365 RBI. He played for six teams and in both leagues, and later served as a scout for the White Sox.

After Orlando retired, his personal life took a wrong turn. Just a year out of baseball, the former slugger was arrested and found guilty of smuggling marijuana into his native Puerto Rico. He served a ten-month prison sentence. That incident caused a rift between Cepeda and his friends and family. In recent years, though, he has been welcomed back by many of those who once shunned him, and he has performed a wide range of substantial community service.

BOB ALLISON—AL 1959

Looking at them now, Bob Allison's minor league statistics provide no clues of what he would do once he donned a major league uniform. But the backs of baseball cards and the like aren't meant as crystal balls, and as a member of the Senators/Twins franchise, Allison proved he had the talent all along.

Bob won the 1959 AL Rookie of the Year honors by hitting .261 with 30 homers and 85 RBI. The Senators' new outfielder also led the league in triples (9) and scored 83 runs.

Allison suffered the dreaded "sophomore jinx" in his second full season with Washington, but rebounded in 1961, the first year for the newly named Minnesota Twins, by knocking in a career-high 105 runs.

Bob Allison at the plate.

He never hit for a high average (although he did reach the .287 mark in 1964), but he did hit a sizable number of homers (yearly totals also included 35, 32, and two 29s) and drive in a lot of runs (he reached the century plateau twice in his career).

He was one of the most popular players ever to wear the Twins uniform, and he played all thirteen of his big-league years with the Senators/Twins franchise.

And even non-Twins fans who saw him make the play will tell you this: Bob's diving, one-handed catch of Jim Lefebvre's booming liner down the left-field line in the fifth inning of Game Two of the 1965 World Series was one of the best ever in postseason play.

WILLIE McCOVEY—NL 1959

It's no stretch to say that "Stretch" may be the most popular player ever to wear the uniform of the San Francisco Giants.

Who is Stretch? His real name is Willie McCovey, and he terrified opposing pitchers as much as any NL hitter of the 1960s and 1970s. He was six feet four inches and 225 lean pounds of power, and he led the National League in home runs three times (he tied for the lead once, with Hank Aaron in 1963), in slugging percentage three times (including .656 in his MVP year, 1969), and in RBI twice. In the same seasons in which he led the league in slugging percentage, he was among the league leaders in drawing walks. It's a safe bet to assume that some of those walks were "unintentionally intentional."

For his inaugural season in the bigs, Willie hit a whopping .354 with 13 homers and 38 RBI to go with his 32 runs scored. If that doesn't sound like much, consider that he put up those numbers in just 192 at-bats over 52 games. For his efforts, he became the second consecutive Giant to win the NL Rookie of the Year Award, and the second consecutive Giant to win it unanimously.

Following a three-year hitch with NL West rival San Diego and a coffee break with the A's in the American League in the mid-1970s, "Stretch" returned to San Francisco for the 1977 season and promptly won Comeback Player of the Year honors after hitting .280 with 28 homers and 86 RBI.

Willie McCovey was named to the Hall of Fame in 1986.

Willie McCovey swings through during the 1969 All-Star Game, in which he socked two home runs to help bring the National League to victory.

"Déjà vu all over again"

Baseball fans in San Francisco and Washington, D.C., must have been mighty proud of their farm systems in the late 1950s. The Giants (with first baseman Orlando Cepeda) and the Senators (with outfielder Albie Pearson) had baseball's top rookies in 1958. These two clubs then repeated the same success the following year with first baseman Willie McCovey and outfielder Bob Allison, respectively. (The Senators traded Pearson early in the 1959 season. The Giants found themselves with a logjam at first base, and wound up alternating Cepeda and McCovey between first base and the outfield for the next several years.)

CHAPTER THREE

THE 1960s

RON HANSEN—AL 1960

Bucky Dent was a great fielder and had a great eye at the plate, but is probably best known for his three-run homer in the 1978 AL East Championship. This home run was essential to the New York Yankees' 5–4 win over the Boston Red Sox, which decided that championship, but Dent once said to an interviewer that he wished people would remember that he also had a good overall career. "For some, that home run's all they remember," Dent said wistfully.

Perhaps Ron Hansen, the AL Rookie of the Year for 1960, has encountered a few folks along the way who recall only that he is one of just eight big-league players to make an unassisted triple play.

Like Dent, Hansen was a light-hitting shortstop as far as yearly and career batting averages go. But unlike Dent, Hansen actually *was* a home-run threat. Hansen was in double figures in home runs in five of his first six seasons—he hit 20 for the 1964 Chicago White Sox as they battled the Yankees in a tight race for the pennant, and 22 in his rookie season with the Baltimore Orioles. Ron Hansen was sort of the Shawon Dunston of his day, an excellent glove man with some pop in his bat, except Hansen had a much better eye at the plate.

In his award-winning rookie season, Ron logged career bests not only in home runs (22) but also in triples (5) and RBI (86). And his totals that year in runs scored (72) and batting average (.255)—when comparing only his full seasons—were second only to the totals that he accumulated in 1964.

Baltimore's Ron Hansen tags home plate to score a run in the sixth inning of the Detroit-Baltimore game on May 21, 1960.

Although he made 29 errors at short that first year, he did lead his fellow AL shortstops in putouts and was second in assists and double plays, behind Chicago's Luis Aparicio. (As an interesting sidelight, these two men replaced each other three years later when Chicago and Baltimore made a trade in early 1963.)

From about 1963 on, Hansen was at or near the top of most defensive categories for AL shortstops. He made his much-ballyhooed unassisted triple play in late July of 1968, in a game against the Cleveland Indians. Ron was playing for the Washington Senators at that point in the season, but was traded back to the White Sox four days later.

FRANK HOWARD—NL 1960

Frank Howard drops his bat and starts for first after hitting a pop fly in the first inning of the Milwaukee–Los Angeles game on July 31, 1960.

Even today, when the television camera pans to the dugout or the coach's box during a ball game before stopping to zoom in on him, broadcasters will call him Big Frank Howard, as if Frank were his middle name.

Howard's playing days have been over for twenty years, but he is still remembered as one of the more fearsome sluggers from the early 1960s through the early 1970s. And "big" doesn't begin to capture Howard's presence at the plate. In his prime, he carried 255 pounds on his six-foot-seven-inch frame. He was the quintessential long-ball hitter: all or nothing at all. He struck out nearly twice as often as he walked (although he led the American League in walks in 1970 with 132), he poked a reasonable number of doubles (five seasons of 20 or more), and twice—in 1962 and 1965—he hit 6 triples.

But it is for his often mammoth shots into the next county that Frank Howard is best remembered. He led the league with 44 dingers in 1968 and again in 1970—the same year in which he led the league in RBI with 126. His 44 homers in 1968 were truly an eye-opening accomplishment when one considers that 1968 was "the year of the pitcher." Batting averages and run production both took a nosedive that season, and pitchers Denny McLain of the Detroit Tigers won 31 games and Bob Gibson of the St. Louis Cardinals crafted a 1.12 earned-run average to go with his 13 shutouts. Want more evidence? Carl Yastrzemski led the American League in batting with a .301 average.

Howard's rookie season was also a dandy. He hit .268 with 23 home runs and 77 RBI in the 117 games in which he appeared for the Los Angeles Dodgers. He scored 54 runs, too. He was named the NL Rookie of the Year for 1960, beating out teammate Tommy Davis and Cubs third baseman Ron Santo for the honor.

Frank played in only one World Series, in 1963, but he made the most of it by smashing a solo homer into the second deck of Dodger Stadium in Game Four to help Los Angeles to a four-game sweep of the Yankees.

"Hondo," as he was called by some (though Big Frank Howard was the moniker that has stuck), played for sixteen years in the majors, then went into coaching and managing.

DON SCHWALL—AL 1961

The Red Sox were a sixth-place team in 1961, but Don Schwall was their ace, and his numbers were good enough to earn him the AL Rookie of the Year Award.

Schwall went 15–7 with a 3.22 ERA, and he pitched 10 complete games. He allowed 167 hits in 179 innings of work and threw 2 shutouts. Don's only debit that year was that he walked too many batters—110 walks against 91 strikeouts.

Control problems plagued him throughout much of his seven-year big-league career, although he did end up fanning a few more batters than he walked. Schwall narrowly carved a winning percentage for himself by going 49–48 with a 3.72 ERA from 1961 through 1967.

Don was traded to Pittsburgh after the 1962 season and was then saddled with the eighth-place Pirates team in 1963. Management used him as both starter and reliever. A 6–12 record with no saves and a 3.33 ERA that year and a 4–3 record with no saves and a 4.35 ERA in 1964 (when the Pirates finished in a sixth-place tie with the Dodgers) indicated that a change was needed. A pitcher can't be all things to all people. So as the 1965 season opened, Don's new role was as a reliever.

Coming out of the bullpen, Schwall won 9 and lost 6 with 4 saves and a much-improved ERA of 2.92. It appeared that he was back on track. Despite his newfound success, however, Schwall found himself standing on the trading block in mid-June of 1966.

Schwall finished his career with the 1966 and 1967 Atlanta Braves. There, he compiled a 3–3 record with a 4.37 ERA—the promise of his rookie season gave way to a less kind reality. Had he pitched for contending teams, Don may have fared much better. He certainly had the right stuff.

Don Schwall looses a curveball in the fifth inning of a 1961 Red Sox–Yankees game at Yankee Stadium.

BILLY WILLIAMS—NL 1961

If anyone could have wrested the title "Mr. Cub" from Ernie Banks, it was Billy Williams. But Billy didn't want the title. That belonged to his longtime buddy in Cub pinstripes.

All Billy ever wanted was respect, and did he ever get it from opposing pitchers. When the smoke cleared after the fire had died out on his eighteen-year major league career, the man dubbed "Sweet Swinging Billy Williams" had clubbed 426 home runs and knocked in close to 1,500 runs. He clubbed 434 career doubles, scored more than 1,400 runs, and hit .290.

Despite a .333 average, 122 RBI, 95 runs scored, 37 homers, 6 triples, and 34 doubles, Billy lost the 1972 NL Most Valuable Player Award to Cincinnati Reds catcher Johnny Bench, who topped Billy's home-run total and his RBI total by 3 but batted 63 points lower than Billy.

Williams never got to play in a World Series, and he was thirty-seven years old by the time he appeared as a designated hitter with the Oakland A's in the 1975 American League Championship series.

Because his popularity and fame were at their greatest in the late 1960s and early 1970s, many people have forgotten that Billy won the NL Rookie of the Year Award for 1961. But his numbers that year—a .278 batting average with 25 home runs and 86 RBI—were the beginning of a pattern that would run throughout his career: run production, home runs, patience, and an excellent eye at the plate for a power hitter (he struck out just one time more than he walked). He also became a solid defensive player in the outfield and at first base.

Billy later served as a batting instructor, coach, and consultant with the Cubs. He was elected to the Hall of Fame in 1987. His induction speech, which included a call for more minority persons in administrative and management positions throughout professional baseball, was eloquent and strong, but never strident.

Billy Williams takes a break for the camera during 1962 spring training.

TOM TRESH—AL 1962

Tom Tresh had the kind of rookie season that dreams are made of.

First, he played for a terrific team—the 1962 Yankees—which won an exciting seven-game World Series over the San Francisco Giants. Second, during the regular season, he did a fine job at shortstop as Tony Kubek's temporary replacement and played in the same outfield with baseball stars Mickey Mantle and Roger Maris. And third, he put together the kind of first full season that cinched his winning the AL Rookie of the Year honors.

Tresh's father, Mike, played for the White Sox and Indians over a twelve-year span in the 1930s and 1940s. But Mike, a catcher, never matched his son's numbers—in 1962 Tom Tresh hit .286 with 20 home runs and 93 RBI while scoring 94 runs and lining 26 doubles and 5 triples into the gaps. With numbers like these, it's not surprising that the BBWAA selected Tom as its AL Rookie of the Year.

Tom hit .321 in the World Series and thrilled the fans at Yankee Stadium when he socked a 3-run homer to win Game Five.

Tresh never repeated the overall success he had experienced during his rookie season, though he did have seasons of 25, 26, and 27 home runs and hit as high as .279 for a season. He closed out his nine-year career in the majors in 1969 as a member of the Tigers.

Tom Tresh and 1951 NL Rookie of the Year Willie Mays take a moment to chat before the first game of the 1962 World Series at Candlestick Park, San Francisco.

KEN HUBBS—NL 1962

In mid-February of 1964, a small plane crashed about five miles outside of Provo, Utah. The pilot and his one passenger were killed. The twenty-two-year-old pilot—Cubs second baseman Ken Hubbs—was the NL Rookie of the Year for 1962.

Hubbs hit .260 that season with 24 doubles, 9 triples, and 5 home runs that fueled his 49 RBI. He also scored 90 runs. He was anything but selective at the plate, striking out a whopping 129 times while taking just 35 walks. His offensive numbers were not quite as good in his second year with the Cubs, but he did hit 3 more home runs. Although Hubbs died before his career had a chance to blossom, observers at the time said he was improving on defense with every game and was starting to learn the strike zone a little better.

Ken's most frequent replacement in the 1964 campaign was Joey Amalfitano, who would later manage the Cubs for three seasons. Amalfitano's replacement in 1965 was Glenn Beckert, who starred at second base for the Cubs through the 1973 season.

Ken Hubbs takes a swing during a 1962 game against the Mets.

GARY PETERS—AL 1963

It may seem ironic that White Sox hurler Gary Peters' worst season was 1968, the so-called year of the pitcher.

On the other hand, White Sox hitters—who knocked in the fewest runs and scored the fewest runs in the American League that year—did their part to make it the "year of the opposing pitcher" by failing to give their own hurlers the necessary run support. Sox fans may well have called it the "year of the pitcher *except* for Gary Peters and a few others."

Otherwise, Peters had a fine fourteen-year career, which he spent with the White Sox and, from 1970 to 1972, with Boston. His 20 wins (the Angels' Dean Chance also won 20) led the American League in 1964, when Chicago's South Siders made a valiant effort to overtake the Yankees down the stretch. Two years later, Peters notched the league's best ERA with a sparkling 1.98.

He also had two years of 16 wins each and twice broke the 200 mark for strikeouts.

But this lefty's personal best may have been his rookie season—1963. That year he won 19 while losing 8, had a league-leading 2.33 ERA, pitched 13 complete games (including 4 shutouts), allowed only 192 hits in 243 innings, gave up only 9 homers, and struck out 189 batters while walking 68.

For that kind of output, it was little wonder that the BBWAA voted Gary the AL Rookie of the Year for 1963.

For his career, Peters went 124–103 with a 3.25 ERA and twice as many strikeouts as walks.

Gary Peters at the mound during 1966 spring training.

PETE ROSE—NL 1963

One of the more endearing aspects of baseball is its ability to bring the generations together, both on the field and in the stands.

When Cardinals legend Stan Musial smacked two singles to right against the Reds in his final game on September 29, 1963, rookie Pete Rose was the Reds' second baseman. It was Rose who, over the course of his long and stellar career, broke some of Musial's NL batting records. Neither man knew it at the time, but it was as if the baton had been passed to the next runner in a generational relay.

Rose's first season in the majors barely hinted at what was to come later. Still, his .273 batting average, 25 doubles, 9 triples, and 6 home runs nicely complemented his 41 RBI and 101 runs scored. Those numbers were good enough for the BBWAA to name the crew-cut dynamo the 1963 NL Rookie of the Year. And Rose was one highly touted rookie who delivered *big* on his initial promise.

Pete's enthusiasm for the game, his play-hard-at-all-costs style, and his knowledge of opposing pitchers helped him become one of the peskiest hitters that baseball has ever known. Almost every baseball fan knows that he is the all-time leader in base hits with 4,256. Less well known, however, is the fact that during his twenty-four-year run in the majors, he walked over 400 times more often than he was struck out.

He is second (behind Hall of Famer Tris Speaker) in career doubles. During the course of Pete's career, he was first—or tied for first—in hits seven times; in runs scored four times; in doubles five times; and in batting average three times. He was in double figures in home runs eight times and triples three times.

Balls hit in his direction didn't often clank off his glove, either, as his season totals in fielding percentage, putouts, and assists indicate.

Pete Rose's selection as the league's top rookie for 1963 was the perfect prelude to the career of one of the game's greatest players.

Pete Rose makes a solid hit during a well-attended game in 1973.

TONY OLIVA—AL 1964

As a fresh-faced young man in his early twenties, Cuban-born Tony Oliva got 4 hits in nine times at bat for a .444 average. That was in 1962. The next year he got 3 hits in seven at-bats for a .429 average. In between those stints with the Minnesota Twins, Tony was hitting .350 with 93 RBI and 17 home runs and .304 with 74 RBI and 23 home runs in the minors.

A ballplayer doesn't get off to a much better start than Oliva did in those formative seasons. But when he made the majors to stay in 1964, Oliva showed just how good he really was. His rookie season remains one of the most impressive big-league debuts of all time. Tony led the league in hitting with a .323 average, in hits with 217—still the AL rookie record—in runs scored with 109, and in doubles with 43. He pasted 32 homers and 9 triples, and he fielded well in the outfield. Tony was the BBWAA's overwhelming choice for 1964 AL Rookie of the Year.

In 1965, he virtually duplicated the success of his rookie season despite a 50 percent drop in his home-run total and a slight decline in total hits. Still, Oliva banged out more hits than anyone else in the American League that year. And his .321 batting average was also tops. In 1966 he led the league in hits for a *third* straight year and again batted over .300.

Tony hit .304 lifetime over a fifteen-year big-league career, the entirety of which he played with Minnesota. Twice he knocked in more than 100 runs for the season on his way to logging 935 career RBI and 329 career doubles. He led the league in hitting three times, hits five times, and doubles three times (in 1970 he tied with teammate Cesar Tovar for most doubles, with 36).

Oliva's seasonal and lifetime numbers undoubtedly would have been even more impressive had he not been plagued by knee injuries throughout his career. Five times he had knee operations. After he retired at the close of the 1976 season, Tony embarked on his second baseball career, that of coach and hitting instructor for the Twins organization.

Tony Oliva displays the form that made him a superstar.

DICK ALLEN—NL 1964

Though moody at times, Dick Allen could carry a team.

He was alternately called "Richie" or "Dick," plus a few other choice names, by teammates and fans alike. As for himself, Richard Anthony "Dick" Allen was a man of action, not words. Over a fifteen-year career in the majors, he let his bat do the talking. And his bat often refused to shut up.

Allen debuted with the Philadelphia Phillies in September 1963. He hit .292 (which would be his career average) and gave team management an indication of what the Pennsylvania powerhouse could do once he had a full season under his belt. Unfortunately, that first full season—1964—was the Phillies' haunted year, when they blew a substantial lead over the rest of the National League and wound up losing the pennant by one game on the last day of the season.

But for Allen, 1964 was a masterpiece. He was named NL Rookie of the Year after he ripped into opposing pitchers for a .318 average, 91 RBI, 29 homers, 38 doubles, and a league-tying 13 triples. He led the league in runs scored with 125, and he cracked 201 hits. About the only thing that made Phillies fans wince was the aftermath of Allen's attempts to field his position at third base: between the boots and the errant throws, his 41 errors led all major league third basemen in 1964.

But what Dick Allen is remembered for is crushing the ball into the bleachers. Dick hit better than .300 seven times, knocked in 90 or more runs six times, and hit more than 30 home runs six times. As a member of the White Sox in the early 1970s, he twice led the American League in home runs and once in RBI. He was named league MVP in 1972 when he hit .308 with 37 homers and 113 RBI. That year, dividing his time between first and third base, Dick made only 7 errors.

CURT BLEFARY—AL 1965

Curt Blefary's rookie card (#49 in the 1965 Topps set) is valued on the open market at about a buck in near-mint condition. But Curt's value to the team for which he played most during his career—the Baltimore Orioles—was much, much greater.

Blefary was a starting outfielder for the 1965 Orioles squad, which finished in third place. In 144 games he hit .260 with 70 RBI, 22 homers, and 23 doubles. He also made only 5 errors. Those numbers were good enough to win him the AL Rookie of the Year Award.

In Baltimore's World Championship season of 1966, Blefary divided his time between the outfield and first base and hit .255 with 64 RBI and 23 home runs. He put up similar home run and batting average totals in 1967, and saw his RBI reach a career high of 81.

Blefary struggled at the plate the following year—in part, perhaps, because he played three vastly different defensive positions: outfield, first base, and catcher. He was traded to the Houston Astros for the 1969 season and enjoyed a good, if not spectacular, year under the dome. He hit .253 with 67 RBI, 26 doubles, a career-high 7 triples, and 12 home runs.

Curt's versatility—he played every position except shortstop and pitcher during his eight-year big-league career—and his occasional home-run power contributed to the successes of five major league teams.

Curt Blefary, shown here in a relaxed moment at the Orioles' spring training camp in March 1965, helped the team earn a World Championship the following year.

JIM LEFEBVRE—NL 1965

Jim Lefebvre hails from the same community—Hawthorne, California—as America's legendary rock band the Beach Boys. And while that band was knocking out hits on the *Billboard* pop charts during the 1960s, Lefebvre was knocking out hits on big-league baseball fields.

Lefebvre played his entire career, from 1965 to 1972, with the Dodgers. Positioned mostly at second and third, Lefebvre was one of those solid, everyday ballplayers who rarely steal the headlines from their teammates but who contribute greatly with the bat and the glove.

As a rookie in 1965, Jim hit .250 with 12 home runs and 21 doubles. This occasional pop in his bat helped him plate 69 runners that year as the Dodgers won the NL pennant and then beat the Twins, four games to three, in a tightly played World Series. In that Series, Jim hit for a .400 average, the best for any player on either team.

But it is on the merit of his regular-season contributions that a young ballplayer is awarded Rookie of the Year honors, and such was the case for Jim in 1965, when he took home the National League's award.

Lefebvre showed himself even better in his sophomore season. He reached career highs in RBI (74), home runs (24), doubles (23), hits (149), runs scored (69), and batting average (.274). Over the years, he didn't sustain that kind of output, but, like his 1965 AL Rookie of the Year counterpart, Curt Blefary, Jim Lefebvre was a smart, reliable ballplayer whose name was usually penciled in on the lineup card before the start of each game.

A baseball man through and through, Jim later served as both coach and manager at the big-league level.

An interesting sidelight to Jim's career is that he was part of the 1965 and 1966 Dodgers' all-switch-hitting infield, which also featured former Rookie of the Year Jim Gilliam, speedster Maury Wills, and future broadcaster Wes Parker.

Jim Lefebvre so loved baseball that he would sometimes sit alone in the ballpark hours before game time and reflect on his profession.

TOMMIE AGEE—AL 1966

Although the New York Mets' surprising win over the favored Orioles in the 1969 World Series has been the subject of much argument, one thing is clear: one of the key reasons for their success was defense.

Mets right fielder Ron Swoboda made the most spectacular defensive play of the Series with his diving catch of a Brooks Robinson liner in the ninth inning of Game Four, but two thrilling plays made by the Mets' Tommie Agee in Game Three were just as crucial to New York's effort.

Agee came up through the Cleveland organization in the early 1960s and was then traded to the White Sox, for whom he put together one very solid season—his rookie season. Never a patient hitter, Tommie struck out 127 times in 1966. Still, when he connected, the score of the game very often changed. That year he hit .273 with 86 RBI, 27 doubles, 22 home runs, 8 triples, and 44 steals. He also scored 98 runs. Agee easily won the BBWAA's accolades as the AL Rookie of the Year for 1966.

His production wasn't nearly as good the next year, and by 1968 Agee found himself playing for a franchise that in its first six years of operation had finished no higher than ninth in a ten-team league. After a horrible first season with the Mets, the Tommie Agee of old resurfaced, and he hit .271 with 76 RBI, a career-high 26 homers, and 97 runs scored for the 1969 Mets.

Agee had two more good seasons at the plate—1970 and 1971—before he played out the string with the Mets, the Astros, and the Cardinals.

Tommie Agee's twelve-year big-league career included Rookie of the Year honors and a World Series ring.

TOMMY HELMS—NL 1966

Infielder Tommy Helms was a superb glove man who was a mainstay for the Reds from 1966 through 1971.

His rookie season was not marked by huge production numbers. Still, Helms hit for a batting average of .284, accumulating 23 doubles, and he drove in 49 runs to go with his career-high 72 runs scored. And though he rarely hit the long ball, Tommy cracked a career-high 9 homers in his debut season. The BBWAA voted him the 1966 NL Rookie of the Year.

As a member of the 1970 Reds, Helms finally got into a World Series, but the Reds were no match for an Orioles team led by a pair of 24-game winners—Mike Cuellar and Dave McNally—and six batters each with 17 or more home runs for the year.

Helms went to the Astros in 1972 and remained with the club until 1976, when he went to the Pirates. He finished his 14-year hitch in the big leagues as a member of the 1977 Red Sox.

Tommy batted .269 lifetime, but as a pinch hitter he hit .290. He was also versatile in the field: he played the lion's share of his games at second, but he also played a number of games at shortstop and third base.

After his playing days were over, Helms served as a coach and a manager. He was at the Reds' helm in late 1989 in the wake of the Pete Rose–Bart Giamatti fiasco.

Tommy Helms' coaching career has matched his playing career for longevity.

ROD CAREW—AL 1967

Had he played in the "dead ball" era preceding the 1920s, Rod Carew might be one of the first players mentioned any time today's fans start talking about baseball's all-time greatest hitters. But Carew played most of his career in the 1970s and 1980s, when home-run giants ruled the land and high-average hitters with little pop in their bats were considered quaint.

The most homers Carew hit in any given year were the 14 he popped in 1975 and 1977 while with the Twins. But make no mistake about it: Carew was a superb hitter. He won seven AL batting titles, including one with a career-high .388 in 1977, when he also led in hits, runs scored, triples, and on-base percentage, and knocked in a career-best 100 runs. He was rightly named league MVP for his accomplishments.

But Carew established himself as a potent offensive weapon long before his MVP year. In 1967, as a twenty-one-year-old kid who had already notched a pair of .300 seasons in the minors, Rod hit .292 with 51 RBI, 22 doubles, 7 triples, and 8 home runs to go with his 66 runs scored. He was the clear choice to receive AL Rookie of the Year honors from the BBWAA.

With his lay-the-bat-on-the-ball, hit-to-all-fields philosophy, Carew amassed more than 3,000 hits in his career, hit over .300 in fifteen of his nineteen years as a major leaguer, and wound up hitting .328 lifetime. In fact, those fifteen years in which he hit over .300 were *consecutive*. Rod was no slouch on defense, either. He played the outfield and all four infield positions, and he also served as designated hitter for part of his career.

You Can Go Home Again . . . And Again . . . and Again . . .

Two players hold the major league record for most steals of home in one season (7), and both had previously won the Rookie of the Year Award. The Brooklyn Dodgers' Pete Reiser, who was the 1941 Rookie of the Year, set the record in 1946, a year in which he also led the majors in total steals, with 34. The Minnesota Twins' Rod Carew, who was the 1967 AL Rookie of the Year, tied the record in 1969, when he also led the league in hitting with a .332 average.

Rod Carew is second only to Hall of Famer Ty Cobb in batting championships.

TOM SEAVER—NL 1967

Tom Seaver's arm made him famous, but his powerful legs were the key to his success.

Whenever legendary pitcher Tom Seaver was interviewed during his playing days, he always exuded that boy-next-door charm. And even today, when he interviews others in his role as a commentator during televised baseball games, he exudes that same charm.

But few boys next door have been able to fire a high fastball toward home plate the way Seaver could in his prime. A control pitcher who could also "smoke 'em inside," Seaver had a winning record in 16 of his 20 big-league seasons, some of them spent with bad teams.

"Tom Terrific," as he came to be known, debuted with the Mets in April 1967 and soon established himself as one of the best young arms to take center stage in a long time. He fashioned a 16–13 record with a 2.76 ERA for a Mets club that wound up in the NL cellar. The only Mets starter with a winning record that year, Tom was the deserving winner of the 1967 NL Rookie of the Year Award.

Seaver's sophomore season echoed his rookie effort, but with two important differences: his ERA dropped by half a run and his strikeout total nudged past the 200 mark.

With a 25–7 record and a 2.21 ERA, Seaver was the ace of the Mets' pitching staff when the team won it all in 1969. In 1973, he and his mates enjoyed dual success again when he went 19–10 with a league-leading 2.08 ERA and 251 strikeouts while the ball club won the NL pennant.

Tom led the National League in ERA three times, in wins three times, and in strikeouts five times. He won three Cy Young awards as best pitcher in the NL. Over in the American League in 1985, toward the end of his long career, he won his 300th career game while playing for the White Sox—on the same day, coincidentally, that the 1967 *AL* Rookie of the Year, Rod Carew, nailed his 3,000th career hit.

Seaver was elected to the Hall of Fame in 1992.

Still, They Had Good Careers

Although Tom Seaver received both Rookie of the Year and Hall of Fame honors, these two forms of praise do not always come together. Not every player who is named Rookie of the Year goes on to a lengthy and successful career, and some players who fail to win the award do go on to bigger and better things. Well-known players who fall into the latter category include several Hall of Famers—Whitey Ford, Hoyt Wilhelm, Al Kaline, Joe Morgan, and Henry Aaron—and several who are either shoo-ins to make the Hall of Fame or have a legitimate chance at making it: Gary Carter, George Brett, Barry Bonds, Ozzie Smith, Ryne Sandberg, Bob Boone, and Wade Boggs.

STAN BAHNSEN—AL 1968

As the 1968 season came to a close, there was little doubt about who would win the AL Rookie of the Year Award.

With a 17–12 record and a cool 2.05 ERA that complemented his 10 complete games, 162 strikeouts, and only 216 hits allowed in 267 innings, Iowa native Stan Bahnsen was the clear choice for the honor.

Bahnsen's record the following year—9–16—mirrored the troubles experienced by his team, the New York Yankees, which finished below .500. But Stan bounced back for the 1970, 1971, and 1972 seasons, the last of which was spent with the White Sox. That year he posted a 21–16 record with a 3.60 ERA and threw twice as many strikeouts as walks.

The 1973 campaign, however, was a tough one for Bahnsen, as he joined such baseball luminaries as Walter Johnson and Steve Carlton—pitchers who notched at least 20 wins in a particular season only to lose at least 20 the next. (Bahnsen still managed to win 18 games, so it wasn't all bad news.)

In all, Stan pitched for six big-league teams over sixteen years. The closest he ever came to pitching in the postseason was in the strike-shortened season of 1981, when he was part of the Montreal Expos' relief corps.

Stan Bahnsen winds up in a 1968 game.

Johnny Bench follows through in a 1977 game against the Phillies.

JOHNNY BENCH—NL 1968

To the current generation of young television viewers who never saw him play, Johnny Bench is best known for pitching spray paint.

But for many others, particularly those who saw him play for the Reds over the course of seventeen years in the majors, he will always be known for catching a baseball.

Bench entered the major league scene late in the 1967 season. He fared poorly at the plate that year, hitting a paltry .163 and whiffing 19 times. But he was the Reds' catcher of the future, and in his rookie season of 1968, he rewarded the front-office faithful by hitting .275 and knocking in 82 runs. He also hit 15 home runs, and his 40 doubles proved that this slugger was no slug. The BBWAA saw fit to name him its NL Rookie of the Year for 1968, making him the third Reds player in six years to win the award.

Johnny's rookie season laid the groundwork for what would become a Hall of Fame career: nearly 1,400 runs driven in; 389 career home runs—most of them as a catcher; two-time league leader in home runs and three-time league leader in RBI; the NL MVP Award in 1970 and 1972; and two World Series rings (for the Reds' back-to-back championships in 1975 and 1976).

Bench's throwing arm was legendary, and his ability to throw out base runners was at times very impressive. This talent—combined with his ability to smother balls in the dirt, call a good game, handle his pitchers well, and knock the stuffing out of the ball—gave rise by the mid-1970s to accolades that Johnny was certainly the era's best catcher and perhaps one of the greatest catchers of all time.

He was named to the Hall of Fame in 1989 and inducted along with Carl Yastrzemski, the acknowledged leader of the Red Sox team that Bench's Reds outlasted in the legendary 1975 World Series.

Did You Know?

Johnny Bench, who went on to a Hall of Fame career, was the first catcher in either league to win the Rookie of the Year Award. He did it, ironically, in 1968—the "Year of the Pitcher"—which featured a decline in batting averages, more than 330 shutouts, an increase in the number of low-scoring ball games, and such stellar pitching accomplishments as Denny McLain's 31–6 record and Bob Gibson's 1.12 ERA. That year, the twenty-year-old Bench hit .275 with 82 RBI, 15 homers, and 40 doubles. Defensively, Bench led NL catchers in putouts and assists.

Lou Piniella was the first designated hitter in World Series play.

LOU PINIELLA—AL 1969

Baseball fans have several different images of Lou Piniella: hot-tempered manager for the Reds; smart-but-lucky right fielder at a key moment in the 1978 playoff game in which the Yankees beat the Red Sox to win the AL East Championship; steady hitter who played an important role on four World Series teams in six short years.

Piniella was, of course, all of these things. But he was also the 1969 AL Rookie of the Year.

Piniella took the circuitous route before gaining success in the big leagues. He debuted with the Orioles in 1964, going 0-for-1 at the plate, but didn't resurface in the majors until 1968, when he went 0-for-5 for the Indians. But a little more seasoning in the minor leagues helped him gain success with the expansion-club Kansas City Royals in 1969.

On opening day, Piniella smashed a double and 3 singles in 5 at-bats as the Royals outlasted the Twins 4–3 in twelve innings.

In 1969 "Sweet Lou," as he has come to be known, knocked in 68 runs and hit .282 with 11 homers, 21 doubles, and 6 triples. This led to his being named AL Rookie of the Year.

Piniella followed up his solid rookie season with an even niftier campaign in 1970, when he hit .301 with 88 RBI, 11 home runs, and 24 doubles. This was, more or less, the pattern throughout Piniella's major league career: he never socked a lot of homers and he never drove in a hundred runs in any one season, but he often hit for a high average and he played professional baseball full-tilt.

He became a student of the game—particularly under manager Billy Martin in New York, where Lou played for more than half of his eighteen-year career—and guided the Reds to a World Championship in 1990 and the Mariners to the AL West crown in 1995. He was named the 1995 AL Manager of the Year.

TED SIZEMORE—NL 1969

Ted Sizemore parlayed his defensive versatility and capability into a twelve-year career in the majors highlighted by his rookie season of 1969.

As a twenty-four-year-old infielder with the Dodgers, Ted hit .271, scored 69 runs, knocked in 46, and spanked 20 doubles. These numbers weren't dazzling, but they were good enough, combined with the promise he showed in the field, for the BBWAA to vote him the National League's top rookie player for 1969.

His extra-base hits and RBI went down in 1970—in large part because he was injured for much of the season— but Sizemore raised his batting average to .306 and continued to show his defensive chops by playing at second, at short, and in the outfield. Apparently, however, that was not enough to keep him in Dodger blue for another year.

Los Angeles traded him to the Cardinals for power-hitting Dick Allen after the 1970 season. Sizemore quickly endeared himself to the fans in St. Louis and remained a Redbird through the 1975 season. During his stay there, he hit as high as .282 and twice hit .264.

Back with the Dodgers in 1976, Sizemore played sparingly, hitting only .241 with 18 RBI and 9 extra-base hits.

But in 1977, with the NL East Champion Phillies, Ted returned to much loftier heights: he hit .281 with 20 doubles and 47 RBI to go with his 64 runs scored. He played most of the season at second base, his best position of the several he played in the major leagues. (Shortstop, third, catcher, and outfield were the others.)

During the 1978 regular season, Sizemore struggled at the plate (again because of injuries), but he did hit .385 for the Phils in a losing cause against his former team, the Dodgers, in the NL Championship series that October.

After a brief stint with the Cubs, Ted completed his big-league career with the Red Sox. He hit .262 lifetime.

Ted Sizemore in 1970, just months after he was named NL Rookie of the Year.

C H A P T E R   F O U R

THE 1970s

THURMAN MUNSON—AL 1970

Thurman Munson cracks a base hit in the early 1970s.

If Johnny Bench was the premier catcher in the National League in the mid-1970s, then Thurman Munson was his AL counterpart.

Munson didn't hit as many home runs as Bench did, but he did hit for a higher average and drive in 100 runs or more in each of three consecutive seasons. Munson was a key factor in the New York Yankees' AL pennant victories in 1976, 1977 and 1978. And, until the Toronto Blue Jays repeated as World Champions in 1993, the 1977 and 1978 Yankees had been the only AL team since 1974 to accomplish that difficult post-season task.

Munson was twenty-two when he debuted with the Yanks in the dog days of 1969. He played in about two dozen games and hit .256 with a pair of triples and 9 runs batted in. He assumed the team's full-time catching duties in 1970 and hit .302 with 53 RBI. Munson cracked only 6 homers all year, but for a catcher he had decent speed, and he legged out 25 doubles and 4 triples. Behind the plate, Munson showed he could be an excellent handler of pitchers, and his 80 assists led all big-league catchers in 1970. He was the clear choice as the AL Rookie of the Year.

Thurman had a couple of so-so years in 1971 and 1972, but his 1973 season dispelled any lingering doubt that some people may have had about his abilities. He logged a .301 batting average, and his season totals of 74 RBI, 80 runs scored, 29 doubles, and 20 home runs were new high-water marks for him. Another off-year followed in 1974, but then Thurman put together three straight 100-RBI, .300-plus campaigns.

His 1976 season brought him further recognition as the league's best overall catcher when he won the AL Most Valuable Player Award with a .302 batting average, 105 RBI, 17 homers, 27 doubles, and 79 runs scored. In the World Series that year, baseball's best backstops met head to head: Johnny Bench hit .533 with a pair of homers and 6 RBI to lead the Cincinatti Reds to a 4-games-to-0 sweep of the Yankees while Munson hit .529 with no homers and 2 RBI. Both men played flawlessly in the field.

Thurman had another solid season in 1977. A .308 batting average and 100 RBI formed the perfect bookends to 18 homers, 28 doubles, and 85 runs scored. He hit .286 with a double, a homer, and 5 RBI in the AL Championship series and .320 in the World Series, which the Yanks won in six over the Los Angeles Dodgers.

Even though his regular-season power numbers took a nosedive in 1978, Munson's 7 RBI and .320 batting average in the World Series helped his team to its second straight championship.

Thurman was the Yankees' team captain when he died while piloting his private plane in Canton, Ohio, on August 2, 1979. To some observers, this tragic ending to the life of a fan favorite echoed the similar fate of former Chicago Cubs second baseman Ken Hubbs fifteen years earlier.

CARL MORTON—NL 1970

Carl Morton pitched for both the Expos and the Braves.

Quite a few ballplayers begin their professional careers at one position but end up playing all or most of their games in the big leagues at another. Carl Morton was such a player.

Morton began as an outfielder in the Atlanta Braves organization in the 1960s, but by the time the Montreal Expos selected him in the 1968 expansion draft, he was pitching himself to a 13–5 record in the minor leagues. His first campaign in the majors was also the Expos' inaugural season: 1969.

Carl's 0–3 record and 4.60 earned-run average gave little hint that he was ready to play at the big-league level. But his determination to succeed, combined with his natural ability, turned things around for him as the 1970 season unfolded. Remember that baseball was in its second year of division play by then, and when the dust had settled on the regular season, Montreal was bringing up the rear in the NL East.

Carl was super for the Expos: he went 18–11 with a 3.60 ERA while pitching 10 complete games, 4 of them shutouts. The one drawback to his rookie season was his wildness: his 125 walks partially offset his 154 strikeouts. Still, 1970 was an exciting and successful campaign for the twenty-six-year-old righty, and the BBWAA decided that 1970 should be an award-winning one as well: Morton was named NL Rookie of the Year.

A reversal of fortune is how one would describe his 1971 season, as he went 10–18 with a 4.80 ERA. And in the following year, a 7–13 record with an ERA hovering near 4.00 was no laughing matter, either. But Morton was traded to Atlanta in time for the 1973 season, and as a Braves starter, he strung together three straight winning seasons. His last year in the majors was 1976, when he went 4–9 for the last-place Braves.

Carl died of a heart attack in 1983 at the age of thirty-nine.

CHRIS CHAMBLISS—AL 1971

Chris Chambliss quietly starred for three different teams in his seventeen-year stint in the majors. The word *quietly* is used because he wasn't flashy, he wasn't controversial, and he wasn't particularly demonstrative on the field. But Chambliss could hit the baseball a mile, drive in runs, field his position, and sometimes make a winner out of an also-ran.

Chambliss made the major leagues in 1971 as a member of the Cleveland Indians—a team that would finish last in the AL East that year. He put together a rookie season that was good enough to earn AL Rookie of the Year honors: a .275 average and 48 RBI to go with 20 doubles and 9 homers. Not a spectacular debut, but a promising one—particularly since he played in only 111 games.

His 1972 stats were similar to 1971's, but he raised his average to .292. He was a line-drive hitter in a position (first base) often thought of as a power hitter's domain. Even in 1975, after his trade to the Yankees, Chris showed little home-run power. But he did reach new single-season highs in RBI (72), doubles (38), and batting average (.304).

The year 1976 was a watershed season for Chambliss, as he nearly doubled his home-run total to 17 and drove in a career-high 96 runs while hitting .293 with 32 doubles and 6 triples. In the AL Championship series against the Kansas City Royals, Chris belted two homers, including a dramatic solo shot off reliever Mark Littell in the bottom of the ninth to win the fifth and final game of the playoffs and propel the Yankees into the World Series.

About the only time the soft-spoken Chambliss "forgot his lines" in the glare of the spotlight was during the 1982 National League Championship series. Playing for the Braves, Chris went 0-for-10 as the Altanta club dropped the best-of-five series to the St. Louis Cardinals. Barring this one less than glorious moment, Chris put together some fine seasons for Atlanta, particularly 1982 and 1983 (he hit a career-high 20 homers in each season). After his career as a player came to an end, Chambliss moved into coaching, with an eye toward managing.

Chris Chambliss readies himself for a pitch.

EARL WILLIAMS—NL 1971

Like a number of former Rookie of the Year Award winners, Earl Williams was unable to sustain the momentum of his debut campaign and create an overall career that was as successful as his rookie season. But when he was seeing the ball well, he could really put a charge into it.

In 1971 he was named the NL's top rookie after he hit .260 with 87 RBI and 33 homers. He nearly duplicated those numbers in his sophomore season when he hit for a .258 average with 87 RBI and 28 homers. He appeared to have a home with the Braves.

Yet Atlanta traded him to Baltimore at the end of the season, and though he poled 22 homers and drove in 83 in 1972, his average dropped to .237. Earl stayed in low double figures in homers and doubles over the next two seasons because by then he had been relegated to part-time service with Baltimore, Atlanta (again), and Montreal.

In about 900 big-league games, Williams hit 138 home runs, played three defensive positions (catcher, first base, and third base), and also served as designated hitter while playing for the Orioles and the Oakland A's.

Earl Williams seemed destined for greatness in 1971.

Carlton Fisk tinkers with the tools of ignorance.

CARLTON FISK—AL 1972

Is Carlton Fisk's baseball legacy his famed use of body English to keep the ball fair at a critical moment in a World Series game? Not if one looks beyond the oft-played clip from Game Six of the 1975 Series.

Fisk put together an admirable big-league career that spanned one change of Sox—from Red to White in early 1981—and 24 seasons.

Carlton broke into the majors late in 1969 with Boston. He struck out twice and went hitless in five at-bats over the course of two games. That feeble showing kept Fisk in the minors for the entire 1970 season, but he did see limited action with Boston in 1971, hitting .313 with a pair of homers and 6 RBI in 14 games. That was more like it, everyone agreed, and when the 1972 season rolled around, Fisk was installed as Boston's starting catcher.

In his rookie season, Carlton hit for a .293 average with 61 RBI, 22 home runs, 28 doubles, 74 runs scored, and a league-leading 9 triples. That was *definitely* more like it, everyone agreed, and the young catcher was named the AL Rookie of the Year for 1972. He was a unanimous choice for the award—the fourth player to hold that distinction up to that point and the first one in the junior circuit.

Various injuries over the course of Fisk's career eroded his playing time in some seasons, but seemed not to erode his skills as a superb handler of pitchers. He could block errant pitches in the dirt as well as any of his contemporaries, and he had a decent throwing arm as well. He also knew precisely how to frame a pitch that was off the plate so that he and his battery mate would get the strike call from the umpire.

His knowledge of the strike zone didn't always follow him to the batter's box, as his yearly strikeout totals and wildly fluctuating batting averages indicate. He hit as low as .221 and .231 and as high as .315 and .331—but again, injuries plagued him throughout his career. Carlton never led in an offensive category except for those 9 triples in his rookie season, but twice he knocked in more than 100 runs for the season, and at the age of thirty-seven he hammered 37 home runs and stole 17 bases for the Chicago White Sox.

After a lengthy public battle between Fisk and White Sox ownership, Fisk was forced to retire before the close of the 1993 season—but not before he established the major league record for total games caught in a career.

No Contest

From 1940 to the present, more than one hundred players have received the Rookie of the Year Award from either the BBWAA's Chicago chapter (1940–1946) or the national organization of the BBWAA (1947–present). Of all those players, only eleven were unanimous selections.

THE AMERICAN LEAGUE

- **Carlton Fisk (1972)**
- **Mark McGwire (1987)**
- **Sandy Alomar Jr. (1990)**
- **Tim Salmon (1993)**

THE NATIONAL LEAGUE

- **Frank Robinson (1956)**
- **Orlando Cepeda (1958)**
- **Willie McCovey (1959)**
- **Vince Coleman (1985)**
- **Benito Santiago (1987)**
- **Mike Piazza (1993)**
- **Raul Mondesi (1994)**

Jon Matlack about to release a pitch.

JON MATLACK—NL 1972

Jon Matlack should have had greater success at the major league level than he did, considering his strikout-to-walk ratio, his complete games, his shutouts, and some very good earned-run averages. But elbow problems, combined with pitching for a few bad teams, have to be factored in.

Jon's introduction to the big leagues was anything but promising. He went 0–3 with a 4.14 ERA for the 1971 New York Mets. The next year, however, he showed his true colors as he won 15 games (against 10 losses) and crafted a 2.32 ERA, the best among Mets starters. In 244 innings of work, he allowed 215 hits and 71 walks while amassing 169 strikeouts.

With numbers like these, it is no surprise that Matlack easily captured the 1972 NL Rookie of the Year Award.

In the Mets' pennant-winning year of 1973, Matlack fell 2 games below .500 despite pitching 14 complete games and posting a 3.20 ERA with 205 strikeouts in 242 innings. He was again 2 games under .500 in 1974, even though he allowed only 221 hits in 265 innings and notched a 2.41 ERA while improving on his strikeout-to-walk ratio. Matlack also led the league in shutouts that year with 7.

He got back on track for the 1975 and 1976 seasons, going 33–22 and pitching 24 complete games during that time. Jon pitched one more year for the Mets—compiling a 7–15 record—before moving to Texas as part of a four-team trade.

As a Ranger in 1978, Matlack enjoyed one of his better campaigns, one that resembled the general success of his rookie and 1976 seasons with the Mets. But from 1979 through 1983 (his final season in the majors), Jon had but one winning season.

Matlack was a better pitcher than his career won-lost record would indicate. His strikeout-to-walk ratio was very good, he etched a 3.18 ERA over his thirteen-year career, and he was the kind of reliable hurler that a team could count on to take the mound every fourth or fifth day. Jon also led the National League in shutouts twice.

Did You Know?

On September 30, 1972, Pittsburgh Pirates legend and eventual Hall of Famer Roberto Clemente cracked a double off the New York Mets' Jon Matlack, the man who a few months later would be named the NL Rookie of the Year. It was Clemente's three-thousandth (and last) regular-season hit of his career.

AL BUMBRY—AL 1973

Had he played a full season and accumulated the requisite number of appearances at the plate, Al Bumbry might well have given the Minnesota Twins' Rod Carew a tough run for the 1973 AL batting crown.

As it was, Bumbry did equal another of Carew's feats by winning the Rookie of the Year Award. Bumbry hit .337 with 34 RBI, 73 runs scored, 7 homers, 15 doubles, and 11 triples, which tied him with Rod Carew for the league lead in that category.

Al was on an Orioles squad that narrowly missed beating Oakland in the AL Championship series for the opportunity to play in the World Series that year.

Bumbry was not your classic power-hitting outfielder. He never hit more than nine homers in any season and his RBI never totaled more than 53 a year. And despite several seasons of low batting averages, Bumbry did reach the .300 level a couple more times in his fourteen-year big-league career. Al was a reliable defensive player who could steal a base for his club when he had to (he had a 73 percent success rate in steals).

Bumbry hit .281 lifetime and played on two World Series teams—the 1979 Orioles, which lost to the Pittsburgh Pirates in seven games, and the 1983 Orioles, which beat the Philadelphia Phillies in five. After he retired from playing, Al became an Orioles coach and hitting instructor.

Al Bumbry takes a good look at an outside pitch as he takes his turn in the batting cage during 1974 spring training.

GARY MATTHEWS—NL 1973

Four teams benefited from Gary Matthews' combined batting and fielding talents, and fans benefited from his joyful enthusiasm for the game.

Matthews came up through the San Francisco Giants organization. He appeared in 20 games toward the end of the 1972 season and hit .290 with 14 RBI and 4 home runs. That in itself was a pretty good start.

But the numbers he put up in his first full season, 1973—an even .300 with 22 doubles, 10 triples, 12 home runs, 58 RBI, and 74 runs scored—were good enough to snare him the NL Rookie of the Year Award.

Matthews never looked back. He usually hit for a decent average, ranging from the .280s to the low .300s for most of his career, and compiled a fair number of doubles, RBI, and home runs each year (although he hit as many as 20 homers only three times in his career).

Gary's on-field enthusiasm and hustle made him a fan favorite wherever he played. He spent five years with the Giants, four with the Braves, three with the Phillies, and three and a half with the Cubs before winding down with the Seattle Mariners in the role of designated hitter.

By the time he was making circus catches and knocking in runs for the 1984 Cubs, he had acquired the nickname "Sarge," and was seen exchanging salutes with the Wrigley faithful in the left-field bleachers.

Gary Matthews takes stock of the pitcher during a 1974 game against the Phillies.

MIKE HARGROVE—AL 1974

Mike Hargrove was a key reason the Rangers made a run at the A's for the 1974 AL West Championship.

Hargrove hit .323 and plated 66 runners. He played a fluid first base. He subbed in the outfield. He served as designated hitter. And while his power numbers weren't high—18 doubles, 6 triples, 4 homers—the young man was often right in the middle of a Rangers rally. Not surprisingly, Mike was named the AL Rookie of the Year for 1974.

The Rangers were an exciting team that season. Their roster included not only the league's top rookie, but also the league MVP, Jeff Burroughs, and the runner-up in the Cy Young voting, Ferguson Jenkins. A former Cub star, Jenkins forged a classy AL debut with a 25–12 record, 29 complete games, and a 2.83 ERA. To top it all off, the team was managed by master strategist Billy Martin.

Hargrove did some mighty good work in his sophomore season, too, when he hit .303 with 62 RBI, 82 runs scored, 11 homers, and 22 doubles.

He always had an excellent eye at the plate. He led the league in walks twice and tallied over 400 more walks than strikeouts in his career.

One of Mike's better offensive seasons was 1977, when he was still with the Rangers. His .305 batting average was fueled by a career-high 18 homers and 28 doubles. He knocked in 69 runs and scored 98 (a career best).

After a five-year stint with the Rangers, Hargrove played briefly for the San Diego Padres before suiting up for the Indians in mid-1979. Nicknamed the "Human Rain Delay" for his constant fidgeting at the batter's box, Mike had three .300 seasons at Cleveland. In 1987 he embarked on a coaching and managing career, and in 1995 he guided the Indians to the AL pennant.

Rangers manager Billy Martin described Mike Hargrove as a "natural hitter."

BAKE McBRIDE—NL 1974

It had been twenty years since a member of the Cardinals organization had copped Rookie of the Year honors, so Bake McBride became an instant hero to Redbird fans around the country when he was selected as the NL's top freshman player for 1974.

The Missouri native batted .309 for a lineup that included Lou Brock, who stole a record-setting 118 bases, and two 20-homer, 100-RBI men, Reggie Smith and Ted Simmons. Add to that the fact that McBride, Brock, and Smith formed the eighth all-.300-hitting outfield in Cardinals history, and one can see why 1974 was great fun for the franchise and its fans despite the Cardinals' being a game and a half behind the Pirates at year's end.

McBride's .309 average was rounded out nicely by his 81 runs scored, 56 RBI, and 30 steals. He also knocked in 56 runs and smacked 30 extra-base hits.

Bake reached the .300 mark for the next three seasons at St. Louis, but was hitting just .262 when he was traded to the Phillies in mid-June of 1977. The trade didn't sit well with Cardinals fans, but Phillies fans said "thank you very much" as McBride's career really took off in Philadelphia over the next four years.

Bake was there in 1980, when the Phillies squeaked past the Houston Astros in the NL Championship series and topped the Royals four games to two in the World Series. Although McBride may have been overshadowed during the regular season by Cy Young Award winner Steve Carlton or by MVP Mike Schmidt, his .309 average, 87 RBI, and 52 extra-base hits were vital to the Phils' success.

Over the course of his career, McBride was not only a skillful hitter but also a speedy, sure-handed outfielder; it was rare that he made an error. His lifetime batting average is .299.

Bake McBride slides into home plate to score a run in the September 27, 1974, Cubs-Cardinals match-up.

Fred Lynn awaits a pitch in a 1979 game against the Yankees.

FRED LYNN—AL 1975

Fred Lynn's big-league career began on such a jaw-dropping note that it's easy to see why nothing short of a Hall of Fame career would have satisfied his fans and critics alike.

He is the only player in baseball history to win the Rookie of the Year Award and the MVP Award in the same season. Here are his numbers for his rookie year of 1975: a .331 batting average; 105 RBI; league-leading totals in runs scored (103), doubles (47), and slugging percentage (.566); 21 home runs, 7 triples, and 10 stolen bases; and a .983 fielding percentage.

In addition, Fred and his Red Sox teammates won the AL Championship and battled the Reds in a World Series that's still talked about. Lynn socked a 3-run homer in the first inning of Game Six—the same game in which teammate Carlton Fisk's solo blast won the twelve-inning thriller.

Had it belonged to anyone else, Lynn's follow-up season of 1976 would have been viewed as a good one: a .314 batting average with 65 RBI to go with 32 doubles, 8 triples, 10 home runs, and 14 steals. But Fred Lynn wasn't just anyone, and even some of his most ardent fans were upset.

But in 129 games in 1977, his average plummeted to .260. Still, his home runs jumped up to 18 and his RBI total edged back up to 76.

Yet 1977 was a far cry from rookie season, and people began to wonder which season reflected the real Fred Lynn. Well, in 1978 and 1979 the real Fred Lynn returned, as he hit .298 with 22 homers, 33 doubles, and 82 RBI in 1978 and a league-leading .333 average with career highs in homers (39) and RBI (122) in 1979.

The 1980 season was his last with Boston. He hit .301, but a broken toe caused him to lose a third of the season, and all his production numbers went south. Fred himself went west, to the California Angels, in a trade that took place prior to the 1981 season. He was then traded to Baltimore before the 1985 season, and he closed out his career with Detroit and San Diego.

Although Fred never quite reached the .300 level again after 1980, he had several productive years from 1982 through 1988, notably in home runs. He bashed more than 20 in *each* of those years. In seventeen seasons, he hit a total of 306 homers, batted .283, and knocked in 1,111 runs.

JOHN MONTEFUSCO—NL 1975

John Montefusco, a pitcher of some note in the 1970s and 1980s, was cleverly renamed "The Count of Montefusco," after the hero of Alexandre Dumas' novel *The Count of Monte Cristo.*

Montefusco enjoyed his best years with his original ball club, the Giants. A lackluster one-month stint in 1974—a 3–2 record with a 4.81 ERA—gave way to a full season that was an unqualified success for the twenty-five-year-old righty. In fact, John had such a good run that the BBWAA chose him as its NL Rookie of the Year honoree for 1975.

The Count went 15–9 that year with a 2.88 ERA. He pitched 10 complete games, including 4 shutouts, and struck out 215 batters while walking only 86. In 243-plus innings, he allowed just 210 hits and gave up fewer than a dozen homers.

Montefusco's won-lost percentage was barely above .500 in his next season, but he lowered his ERA to 2.84 and accumulated 6 shutouts to tie the Mets' Jon Matlack for the league lead.

Several painful injuries contributed to losing records in three of the next four years, and Montefusco was traded to Atlanta before the strike-shortened 1981 season. Used mostly in relief, he was 2–3 with a save.

Through free agency, John found himself with the Padres for the 1982 season. He went 10–11 that year and 9–4 the next for the Padres before being traded in mid-season to the Yankees. He pitched very well for the pinstripers, winning all five of his decisions and compiling a 3.32 ERA. His last season of note was 1984, when he went 5–3 with a 3.58 ERA for the Yankees.

Noted Dodger-hater John Montefusco had many great games against the Los Angeles team.

MARK FIDRYCH—AL 1976

A lot of Tigers players have been idolized by the Detroit faithful over the years—Ty Cobb, Hal Newhouser, Hank Greenberg, Lou Whitaker, Al Kaline, and Cecil Fielder, to name a few—but none has captured the fans' imagination the way Mark Fidrych did in 1976.

To some observers, he was, in the vernacular, a "flake." He performed several rituals on and around the pitcher's mound, including gripping the ball and scolding it for allowing itself to be hit through the hole for a base hit. His physical appearance—he was six foot three inches and 175 pounds beneath a pile of curly golden hair—brought him the nickname "Big Bird" or "The Bird," after the popular character from the television show *Sesame Street.*

But the fact that Fidrych could pitch a great game wasn't lost on either the fans or the media. In a season when the ballclub struggled to a fifth-place finish in the AL East, "The Bird" was a breath of fresh air.

He won 19 games against just 9 losses, forged a league-leading 2.34 ERA, and led the league in complete games with a phenomenal 24. He didn't strike out many batters (97), but he was stingy with his hits (217 allowed in 250 innings). Fidrych was the overwhelming choice as AL Rookie of the Year for 1976.

Tendonitis eventually got the better of Fidrych when he tried to repeat the success of his rookie season, and he struggled to compile a 10–10 record over the next four seasons before calling it quits. Still, for one glorious season, Mark Fidrych was a terrific pitcher and a great deal of fun to watch—unless, of course, you were rooting for another AL team.

Mark Fidrych was once quoted as saying, "Sometimes I get lazy and let the dishes stack up. But they don't stack too high. I've only got four dishes."

PAT ZACHRY AND BUTCH METZGER—NL 1976

Starting pitcher Pat Zachry fires one down the pike in the third game of the 1976 World Series, in which the the Reds were pitted against the Yankees.

Butch Metzger in 1975, a season away from his Rookie of the Year campaign.

In light of the publicity that arose following his team's repeat as NL West Division champs, it wasn't surprising that the Reds' young pitching sensation, Pat Zachry, was a top vote-getter in the balloting for the league's Rookie of the Year Award. He was, in fact, instrumental in the Reds' success that year, so he was in the glare of the spotlight a lot.

But Butch Metzger was something of a surprise. His team, the fifth-place Padres, was a big reason the Reds won the division by 10 games. Yet Metzger performed splendidly as the bullpen ace for the lowly Padres. He had an 11–4 record with 16 saves (fourth in the league that year) and a 2.92 ERA.

Pat Zachry's 2.74 ERA was fifth-best in the league, and his 14–7 record and 170 hits allowed in 204 innings weren't too shabby, either.

For their efforts, Zachry and Metzger were named co-winners of the 1976 NL Rookie of the Year Award. (This was the first time there had been a tie in Rookie of the Year voting since the award was created in 1940, and it would not be the last.)

Metzger had pitched sparingly for the Giants in 1974 and the Padres in 1975, and he pitched nearly as sparingly over the two seasons following his award-winning rookie campaign before calling it a career. He logged an 18–9 lifetime record and saved 23 games.

Zachry continued to pitch through the 1985 season, spending his entire career in the National League. He switched to the bullpen full-time by 1983. Of the more than 100 contests in which he appeared from 1983 through 1985, he started only one game—which he won. He capped off his rookie season by winning Game Three of the 1976 World Series as the Reds swept the Yankees in four. Coincidentally, Zachry and Metzger were teammates on the 1978 Mets.

EDDIE MURRAY—AL 1977

Eddie Murray has put together what many observers consider a sure Hall of Fame career. His lifetime batting average is close to .300. He has socked well over 400 homers and knocked in more than 1,600 runs. Over the span of his more than 2,600 games, he has scored more than 1,400 runs.

He has reached the 100-plus plateau in RBI six times. Only once in his first dozen big-league seasons did he fail to hit at least 22 home runs; that came in his injury-plagued 1986 campaign, but he still plated 84 runners and hit .305. And far from being one-dimensional, Eddie has played a superb first base over the years.

Murray debuted with the Orioles—the team with which he is most closely associated—in 1977. All he did as a fresh-faced kid was bat .283, blast 27 home runs, bang out 29 doubles, knock in 88 runs, and score another 81 runs. Simply put, Murray hit the ground running and never looked back. He was named the 1977 AL Rookie of the Year and has built on that initial success with each passing year. Eddie holds or shares a number of career and single-season records for switch-hitters, the AL career record for the most game-winning RBI, and the NL single-season record for the most double plays by a first baseman (in 150 or more games)—88—which he tallied in 1990 as a member of the Dodgers.

Still going strong with Cleveland in 1994 (21 doubles, 17 home runs, and 76 RBI) and in 1995 (.323, 21 homers, and 82 RBI), Murray will be a worthy addition to the Baseball Hall of Fame.

Throughout his great career, Eddie Murray in the field has been overshadowed by Eddie Murray at the plate.

Andre Dawson hustling around the bases in 1982.

ANDRE DAWSON—NL 1977

Andre Dawson may be known as much for his knee injuries and resulting surgical operations as for his home-run power, cannonlike arm, and on-field leadership.

But physical maladies don't bring fame and fortune in the world of professional baseball. Physical prowess does. And Dawson has displayed plenty of that in the course of his major league career.

The Expos organization brought him up from the minors toward the end of the 1976 season. In two dozen games, Dawson hit an anemic .235 with no homers and 7 RBI. But the next year, the *real* Andre Dawson showed himself: in 139 games, he hit .282 with 26 doubles, 9 triples, and 19 homers on his way to driving in 65 runs and scoring another 64. At the age of twenty-three, Dawson became the 1977 NL Rookie of the Year.

Andre played for the Expos for 11 seasons before joining the Cubs as a free agent in 1987. Playing for the East Division's cellar dweller, Dawson batted .287, hit 49 homers and knocked in 137 runs to win the league's MVP Award.

Even by his mid- to late thirties, in the twilight of his career, Andre was knocking in 100 runs or more a season and smashing as many as 27 to 31 home runs. But the Cubs eventually elected not to sign him again when his contract ran out, and by 1993 he was playing in the American League. It was as a member of the Red Sox that Andre hit his 400th career home run. Before suffering a season-ending leg injury in 1994, Andre had whacked 16 homers and plated 48 runners as a DH for Boston. In 47 games with the Florida Marlins in 1995, he managed to hit half that many homers to go with 37 RBI.

LOU WHITAKER—AL 1978

Lou Whitaker watches the ball go as he breaks for first base.

Chants of "Lou! Lou! Lou!" have permeated the air in Tiger Stadium for more than 15 years now, and for good reason. All-Star second baseman Lou Whitaker has been a fan favorite practically since he first donned a Tigers jersey in 1977.

Whitaker really got the crowd on his side in the 1978 season, when he batted .285 with 58 RBI and 71 runs scored in 139 games. Selected as the AL's top rookie that year, Whitaker has been a steady player for Detroit throughout his career and formed—with shortstop Alan Trammell—one of baseball's steadiest up-the-middle combos of the 1980s. (The fact that the pair could also hit a little didn't hurt.)

Lou was a big reason the Tigers reached the World Series in 1984. That year he hit .289 with 56 RBI and 90 runs scored plus 13 home runs and 25 doubles.

Whitaker has pasted as many as 20 homers or more in a season, but he has been best known as a consistent glove man and a reliable hitter with a good eye at the plate and an occasional pop in his bat. Talented newcomers Travis Fryman and Chris Gomez have assumed many of Alan Trammell's shortstop duties, but Trammell and Lou Whitaker are still baseball's longest-running double-play combo. Lou's 1994 stats included a .301 batting average, 21 doubles, 12 home runs, and 43 RBI. He hit .293 with 14 homers in 1995.

BOB HORNER—NL 1978

A shoulder injury in late June of 1987 finally got the best of Bob Horner, but even so, he enjoyed a memorable big-league career.

Horner was a power-hitting third baseman for the Braves from the time of his debut as a rookie. He showed so much promise by the time he was twenty that he never played a day in the minors.

After being named 1978's College Player of the Year by *The Sporting News*, Horner signed with the Braves and debuted with the ball club in June of 1978. One wonders what he might have accomplished had he played a full season.

But what a half-season it was! Bob hit .266 and drove in 63 runs while belting 23 baseballs out of NL ballparks. He hit 17 doubles and scored 50 runs. The BBWAA selected Horner as the 1978 NL Rookie of the Year.

At close to 200 pounds, Horner didn't have the greatest range at third (or first, where he played much of the time toward the end of his career), but he had soft hands and a good arm, and besides, when you hit 20 to 35 home runs in less than a season, year in and year out, you don't have to make your living with the leather.

The most games Horner played in any one season were 140 in 1982, when the Braves won the NL West Division Championship, and 141 in 1986.

Bob retired following the 1988 season after nine seasons with the Braves and one with the Cardinals. He also played a year in Japan.

Bob Horner connects in a late-1970s game against the Mets.

ALFREDO GRIFFIN AND JOHN CASTINO—AL 1979

Alfredo Griffin about to drop his bat and make for first base.

John Castino puts the sweet spot to the ball.

In 1976, the National League found itself with a pair of Rookie of the Year honorees—both pitchers. Three years later, the American League wound up with two of its own Rookie of the Year honorees—both infielders.

Blue Jays shortstop Alfredo Griffin hit .287 with 22 doubles, 10 triples, 81 runs scored, and 21 stolen bases. He brought some speed and a lot of excitement to a mostly lackluster lineup that, along with a struggling pitching staff, managed to finish last in the AL East.

Third baseman John Castino played for an also-ran that year as well—the Minnesota Twins, who finished fourth in the AL West. Castino had only 26 extra-base hits (Griffin had 34), but Castino hit .285 and his 52 RBI were 21 more than his co-winner had for the year.

Because both of these players had similarly outstanding debuts, the BBWAA voters decided that both men were good enough to win the 1979 AL Rookie of the Year Award.

Castino put together several more good years with the Twins. He hit .302 with 64 RBI and 13 homers in 1980, led the league in triples in 1981 with 9, and hit .277 with 57 RBI, 11 homers, and 30 doubles in 1983. He suffered a back injury during the 1984 season, and by 1985 he was out of baseball.

Griffin was still active in the big leagues after nearly twenty years of service. He has had mixed success over the years, putting up some pretty good offensive numbers for the A's from 1985 through 1987. Although he has worn the uniforms of several teams (including the Indians from 1976 to 1978), he managed to be in the right place at the right time for the 1992 and 1993 seasons: among the celebrants who captured back-to-back World Championships—the Blue Jays.

RICK SUTCLIFFE—NL 1979

Rick Sutcliffe did have a baseball life before his 16–1, Cy Young Award–winning season of 1984, but don't try to convince Cubs fans of that fact.

It is true, though, and longtime Sutcliffe followers will point to his rookie season as proof. Rick made a few appearances with the Dodgers between 1976 and 1978, but his career finally got going in 1979. That year, he went 17–10 with a 3.46 ERA and allowed only 217 hits in the 242 innings he pitched. For his efforts, Rick won the NL Rookie of the Year honors for 1979 and would be the first of four consecutive Dodgers to win the award.

Interestingly, Sutcliffe was used mostly in relief during the 1980 campaign despite his success as a starter the year before. He struggled to a 3–9 record while his ERA ballooned to 5.56. After he logged a 2–2 record and 4.02 ERA for the strike-shortened 1981 season, the Dodgers sent him to the AL city of Cleveland in a trade that Indians fans soon found to their liking. Rick molded a league-leading 2.96 ERA that year that nicely complemented his 14–8 record. He followed that success with a solid 17–11 record in 1983 even though his ERA zoomed past 4.00.

By mid-June of 1984, Rick was in a Cubs uniform and leading the North Siders to their first postseason appearance in nearly forty years. He had two more good seasons at Chicago (narrowly missing the Cy Young Award in 1987) before he returned to the American League and joined the Orioles' starting rotation. At Baltimore he went 16–15 in 1992 and 10–10 in 1993. He signed with the Cardinals for 1994, a season that both he (6–4, 6.52 ERA) and the team (53–61) would just as soon forget.

Repeat After Me

Several teams have enjoyed having back-to-back Rookie of the Year winners, but the Los Angeles Dodgers can boast of *twice* having four consecutive winners. Rick Sutcliffe, Steve Howe, Fernando Valenzuela, and Steve Sax won the award from 1979 to 1982. Eric Karros, Mike Piazza, Raul Mondesi, and Hideo Nomo repeated the feat from 1992 to 1995. Oakland rookies, by the way, won the AL award three consecutive years, when Jose Canseco, Mark McGwire, and Walt Weiss accomplished a three-peat from 1986 through 1988.

Rick Sutcliffe shows his patented hidden-ball trick just before he whiffs another batter.

CHAPTER FIVE

THE 1980s

JOE CHARBONEAU—AL 1980

From the front office to the players on the field, baseball has long had its eccentrics. Joe Charboneau was one of them.

Dubbed "Super Joe" for his onslaught against AL pitching in 1980, Charboneau was rumored to have used a razor blade to remove a tattoo from his arm and to have performed a root canal on himself with the aid of a pair of pliers. Whether these tales—and those of him opening a beer bottle with his eye socket—are evidence of a deeply troubled individual or simply someone given to extreme forms of horseplay, they can't take away from the fact that Joe put together a whale of a year in 1980.

Joe Charboneau got to the majors after strong back-to-back seasons in the minors, each time leading his league in batting average: .350 at Visalia in 1978 and .352 at Chattanooga in 1979. By that time, Joe was in the Cleveland Indians organization and ready for the big show.

He didn't disappoint. In just 131 games, the good-natured kid hit .289 with 87 runs batted in, 76 runs scored, 23 homers, and 17 doubles. Joe played the outfield well if not spectacularly and seemed destined for stardom when the BBWAA voted him the AL Rookie of the Year for 1980.

Super Joe proved to be a one-season wonder, however, and by 1982 he was back with Chattanooga playing Double-A ball. His last major appearance in a big-league uniform was in 1984, as a member of the New York Knights in the hit motion picture *The Natural*.

In August 1994, *USA Today Baseball Weekly* reported that Charboneau had won a broadcast Emmy for *The Joe Charboneau Series*, a weekly three-minute segment that was a mix of moving and light-hearted sports stories. The series was aired by the CBS affiliate in Cleveland.

Super Joe Charboneau goes for broke.

STEVE HOWE—NL 1980

That Steve Howe was still pitching in the major leagues more than a dozen years after he debuted in a Los Angeles Dodgers uniform is both a testament to his ability to get people out and an example of baseball's puzzling willingness to let him stay in. It seems particularly odd to forgive Howe's repeated drug-related transgressions at a time when public outcry on the social ill has never been louder.

Steve had talent to burn when he arrived on the major league scene as a twenty-two-year-old rookie for Los Angeles in 1980. With a starting rotation of Burt Hooton, Jerry Reuss, Bob Welch, Dave Goltz, and Don Sutton, the Dodgers had the luxury of using Howe out of the bullpen. Although it is certainly not unheard of for a ball club to use a young hurler's talents in relief, the pressure of being a closer can take a large toll on even the most seasoned veteran.

But Howe thrived as the Dodgers' bullpen ace; he saved 17 games with a 2.65 earned-run average and posted a 7–9 won-lost record. The confident kid from Pontiac, Michigan, did all this while his team battled the Houston Astros in a thrilling race for the NL West Championship, which the Astros finally claimed when they beat the Dodgers in a one-game playoff.

Howe was named the league's Rookie of the Year, becoming the second of four consecutive Dodger newcomers to earn that distinction.

Although the Dodgers didn't make it to postseason play in Steve's rookie season, they were crowned World Champions after they bested the Yankees in the 1981 Fall Classic. Steve won Game Four and saved Game Six of that Series.

Howe's continuing battle with drugs, particularly cocaine, became evident to others—if not to himself—as early as his rookie season, and by late 1982, once the season was over, he began the first of what became a sad series of unsuccessful treatments for substance abuse. At one point, Howe was persona non grata as far as Major League Baseball was concerned, and by the late 1980s he was reduced to playing semiprofessional ball in southern California.

Amazingly, Howe has managed to keep his once-promising big-league career afloat, despite several suspensions from the game and a lifetime's worth of bad publicity and broken promises to friends, family, and teammates.

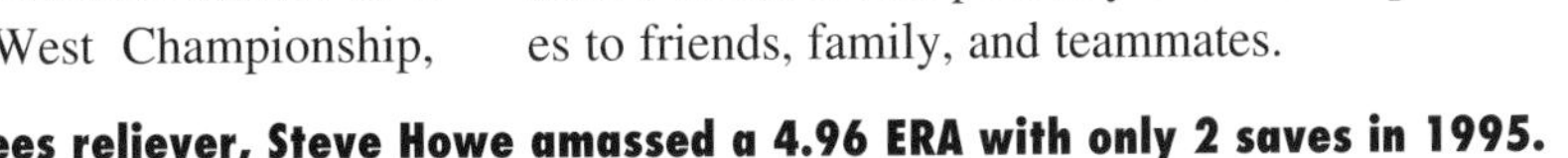

As a Yankees reliever, Steve Howe amassed a 4.96 ERA with only 2 saves in 1995.

Dave Righetti about to release a pitch.

DAVE RIGHETTI—AL 1981

Dave Righetti was a top-flight relief pitcher for much of the 1980s and 1990s, but he won the 1981 AL Rookie of the Year Award for his starting pitching.

In that strike-shortened season, Dave went 8–4 for the New York Yankees with a sparkling 2.06 ERA. He allowed only 75 hits in 105 innings and struck out 89 batters while walking only 38.

Although Righetti made a poor showing in the 1981 World Series, he was key to the Yankees' getting to the October Classic in the first place: he won two games in the divisional playoffs and another in the AL Championship series.

His total bases on balls jumped dramatically the next year (a league-leading 108), as did his ERA (3.79), but so did his strikeouts (163), as he went 11–10 for a sub-.500 Yankees team.

Both Righetti (14–8, 3.44 ERA) and the Yanks (91–71) bounced back in 1983. The season was highlighted by Dave's no-hitter against archrival Boston on July 4 at Yankee Stadium.

Righetti was made a reliever for the 1984 campaign, and it has been in this role that he has enjoyed his greatest success. His 46 saves in 1986 led all relievers that year.

By the early 1990s, Dave was a reliever in the National League, but by 1994 he found himself in the minors, eyeing a return to form and to the big leagues after being released by both the Giants and their Bay Area brethren, the A's, within a six-month period. Righetti eventually signed with the Toronto Blue Jays, for whom he went 0–1 with 10.18 ERA and no saves. He went 3–2 as a starter for the White Sox in 1995.

FERNANDO VALENZUELA—NL 1981

On April 9, 1981, a twenty-year-old rookie pitcher for the Dodgers pitched a 2–0 shutout of the Astros in his first big-league start. It was a glimpse of what was to become a laudable year-long effort by the kid, and helped counterbalance the frustration and anger—felt by everyone who loved the sport—that resulted from seven weeks without baseball because of the strike voted by the Major League Baseball Players Association.

Fernando Valenzuela, who was learning to speak essential English words and phrases at the same time he was learning the weaknesses of opposing hitters, went 13–7 for Los Angeles.

His was not an eye-opening record, but what came with it certainly was. He led the league in complete games (11), shutouts (8), innings pitched (192), and strikeouts (180). At the plate, he batted a nifty (for pitchers) .250. The Mexican-born hurler outdistanced the Montreal Expos' Tim Raines in the voting for the NL Rookie of the Year Award, giving the Dodgers their third consecutive winner. Fernando also snagged the league's Cy Young Award.

To top off his rookie campaign, Valenzuela won a game in the divisional playoffs, a game in the NL Championship series, and a game in the World Series.

The 1982 season was a quality follow-up. Fernando won 19 games against 13 losses, completed 18 of his 37 starts, and compiled a 2.87 earned-run average.

He continued to rack up a lot of innings and a lot of strikeouts for the Dodgers over the next few years. He added a 20-win season to his career record when he went 21–11 with a 3.14 ERA in 1986. That year he led the majors in complete games with 20—a whopping total for this day and age of relief specialists.

By the early 1990s, Valenzuela was in the American League, taking the mound for the California Angels and, later, the Baltimore Orioles. Shoulder problems hampered his ability to pitch as well as he once did, but with the Orioles in 1993 he showed that he could still throw his patented screwball even if he lacks a blazing fastball. He was 1–2 with the 1994 Phillies but 8–3 with the 1995 Padres.

Fernando Valenzuela on the mound in 1989.

Did You Know?

Fernando Valenzuela is the only player to win the Rookie of the Year Award and the Cy Young Award in the same season. He did it in 1981 with the Los Angeles Dodgers.

CAL RIPKEN JR.—AL 1982

Bragging Rights

Which major league franchise has had the most Rookie of the Year honorees? Through the 1995 season, the Dodgers were tops with sixteen. The New York Yankees were second with eight. The Baltimore Orioles—if you count the club's previous incarnation as the St. Louis Browns—were third with seven. The St. Louis Cardinals, the Cincinnati Reds, and the Giants each had six. As the 1996 season opened, three clubs—the Pittsburgh Pirates, the Colorado Rockies, and the Florida Marlins—were still without bragging rights.

Whenever people talk about Cal Ripken Jr., all they talk about is "the record." Ripken has nothing and no one to blame for that but his own talent, his durability, and his perseverance, all of which combined to fuel his highly publicized run at Lou Gehrig's lifetime record of playing in 2,130 consecutive games—which he broke in 1995.

Junior's big-league career has had other key elements going for it, beginning with his award-winning rookie season of 1982. Moving from third base to shortstop, where he still plays, Ripken hit .264 with 93 RBI, 28 home runs, 32 doubles, and 90 runs scored. The BBWAA named him the AL's No. 1 rookie of 1982.

The following year was even better for the budding superstar. He hit .318 with 102 RBI and league-leading totals in runs scored (121), hits (211), and doubles (47). He was becoming a solid defensive shortstop, too, leading his contemporaries in assists and double plays turned. He was named AL Most Valuable Player for his regular-season output and capped the 1983 season by playing errorless ball for the Orioles as they topped the Philadelphia Phillies in the World Series.

Ripken's yearly batting averages dropped steadily after 1987, and he was roundly criticized for his determination to stay in the lineup in order to preserve the streak. But he rebounded dramatically in the 1991 season, hitting .323 with 34 homers and 114 RBI. He also roped 46 doubles and scored 99 runs. For his efforts, he was awarded his second league MVP title.

In 1992, Ripken hit only .251 with 14 homers and 72 RBI. In 1993 he improved greatly on his run production—with 90 RBI and 24 homers—but his batting average floundered in the .250s again.

In 1994, he was on track to have his best overall season since 1991, until the players' strike brought the season to an abrupt stop. Cal wound up with a .315 batting average, 75 RBI, and 13 homers.

Cal broke the Iron Horse's 56-year-old record on the night of September 6, 1995, before a packed house at Camden Yards and a nationwide television audience. For many fans, it was the defining moment in big-league baseball's season-long attempt to return to grace.

Cal Ripken Jr. mans his post at shortstop in a 1988 game against the White Sox.

STEVE SAX—NL 1982

Dodgers second baseman Steve Sax was known for making one bad throw after another to whomever was playing first base—which may have turned manager Tommy LaSorda's hair whiter by the minute—but there's no denying that the otherwise talented young infielder struggled in the field.

During his eight seasons with Los Angeles, Sax hit well, hustled on offense and defense, stole a lot of bases, and generally served as a spark plug for a Dodgers club that made it to the postseason on several occasions. As a second baseman, however, Sax was all too often an errant throw waiting to happen. As a Dodger, he had seasons of 21 and 30 errors, the latter a league high in that department.

But Sax, a tough-as-nails ballplayer, put together some solid years with Los Angeles, including his rookie campaign of 1982, when he became the fourth consecutive player wearing Dodger blue to capture NL Rookie of the Year honors.

Steve hit for an average of .282, knocked in 47 runs, and scored 88 runs to go with his 23 doubles, 7 triples, and 4 home runs. He also swiped 49 bases, which placed him fifth among the league leaders in that category.

As a table-setter for the Dodgers' lineup, Steve was rarely in the position to drive in a lot of runs, but he was a fairly reliable contact hitter who made things happen with his bat and his legs. His best overall season at the plate was 1986, when he hit .332 with 43 doubles, 91 runs scored, 56 RBI, 6 homers, and 40 steals, and put together a twenty-five-game hitting streak.

In 1988, Steve's last season with Los Angeles, he hit an even .300 in the World Series as the Dodgers beat the favored Oakland Athletics four games to one. Despite Sax's throwing problems early in his career, he has played errorless ball in four NL Championship series, one AL Championship series, two World Series, and one division series. His defense has improved over the years, and in 1989, his first year with the Yankees, he led the American League in fielding percentage and double plays turned. As the 1990s hit midstride, Sax found himself in a backup role for the Chicago White Sox and the Oakland A's. Immediately following the 1994 season, Steve announced his free agency.

Steve Sax about to break into a run around the bases.

RON KITTLE—AL 1983

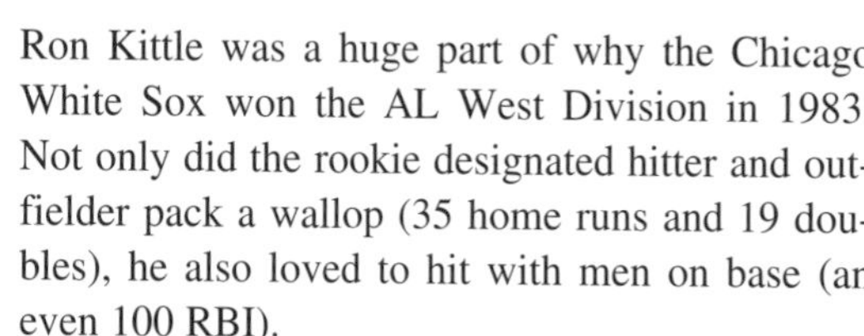

Ron Kittle was a huge part of why the Chicago White Sox won the AL West Division in 1983. Not only did the rookie designated hitter and outfielder pack a wallop (35 home runs and 19 doubles), he also loved to hit with men on base (an even 100 RBI).

Ron also scored 75 runs and managed to advance his six-foot-four-inch, 200-pound frame to the next base eight times in eleven tries. He did all of that in just 145 games.

The only rap against Kittle was that he struck out often (150 times in 520 at-bats), which contributed to a .254 batting average. With Kittle, it seemed, it was all or nothing. Nevertheless, his accomplishments far outweighed his failures, and he was named the league's top rookie for 1983 by the BBWAA.

Kittle continued to hit a lot of home runs for the White Sox over the next three years—75 altogether. But he also continued to strike out a lot and his batting average never got as high as .250 again. He was traded to the Yankees during the 1986 season.

Between 1987 and the early 1990s, Ron bounced around from one AL team to another, finally ending up with the White Sox for a third tour of duty. In 1989, during his second stint with the White Sox, Kittle hit .302 with 11 homers and 37 RBI in just 51 games, but a bad back greatly reduced his playing time.

Ron Kittle goes for a home run.

DARRYL STRAWBERRY—NL 1983

Most New York Mets fans in the 1980s loved him. Opposing teams' fans rode him every chance they got with chants of "Dair-r-ruhl," "Dair-r-ruhl."

But by the mid-1990s, Darryl Strawberry was no longer a Met; he was his own worst enemy because of personal problems and embarrassing public statements, and few people seemed to care when he took his stance in the batter's box.

The simple truth is, the love-me-or-hate-me outfielder showed he was a big-league slugger right from the start. In 1983, the twenty-one-year-old rookie's 26 homers, 15 doubles, and 7 triples powered his 74 RBI. All of that—combined with his 19 stolen bases and 63 runs scored—easily overshadowed his .257 batting average, and Strawberry copped the NL Rookie of the Year Award. It was the first time in five years that someone other than a Dodger had won the award.

Strawberry did even better the next year, when he increased his RBI total to 97, his runs scored to 75, and his doubles to 27. And though he still struck out a lot (128 times in his rookie season, 131 times in 1984), Darryl's eye at the plate was improving some—75 walks in 1984 compared with 47 in 1983—although his batting average actually dipped six points.

He was hampered by a hand injury in 1985, when the Mets chased the St. Louis Cardinals for the East Division title, but he still hit .277 with 79 RBI and 29 home runs. Three of those home runs came in a game against the Chicago Cubs at Wrigley Field in August. Cubs fans gave him their rendition of the "Dair-r-ruhl" chant each time he stepped to the plate, and booed him after each of his first two home runs. They did the same after home run No. 3, but by the time he rounded second base, many Cubs fans actually cheered him for his achievement.

For the 1986 season, Strawberry hit just .259, but knocked in 93 runs with 27 homers and 27 doubles to help the Mets reach postseason play for the first time in more than a dozen years.

Darryl put together his finest campaign in 1987. He hit .284 with 104 RBI, 108 runs scored, 39 homers, 32 doubles, and 36 stolen bases.

In 1988, another good year for him at the plate, he again hit 39 homers (which led the league) and both drove in and scored 101 runs. He also led the league in slugging percentage with a .545 mark.

In 1989, Strawberry's average crashed to .225, but he still socked 29 homers and 26 doubles in 134 games. He came back strong in 1990 when he hit .277 with 37 home runs and 108 RBI.

Darryl Strawberry has often been his own toughest opponent.

Darryl Strawberry has been plagued by various injuries throughout his career, and lately he has also begun showing signs of emotional problems. But when he is healthy, he still wields a powerful bat in any lineup. In 1991, he began playing for the Dodgers in his hometown of Los Angeles. Days before the start of the 1994 season, Strawberry admitted to substance abuse problems and was released by the Dodgers. West Coast rival San Francisco signed him prior to the All-Star break. After joining the Giants, Darryl appeared to turn his life around. Though he never matched his earlier successes, he did well with his new team, knocking out a few home runs and generally playing a good game, and was given a lot of credit by the media. He saw limited action with the Yankees in 1995.

ALVIN DAVIS—AL 1984

Alvin Davis was a teenager when the Seattle Mariners franchise first took the field in the spring of 1977. Seven years later, he became the team's star first baseman and garnered AL Rookie of the Year honors.

Davis went 2-for-3 with an RBI in his lone game at the Triple-A level before being brought up to Seattle in April 1984. A sure-handed fielder in the minors, Davis quickly proved he was a top-notch first baseman at the major league level. Club officials knew the young man could hit, too, but even they must have been surprised with just how good their new first baseman was at the plate.

In his rookie season, Alvin knocked in 116 runs and scored 80. He hit a solid .284 with 27 home runs and 34 doubles. And for a new kid, he displayed tremendous patience at the plate by walking 97 times and striking out just 78 times. Despite good seasons from a few other newcomers, he was the clear choice for AL Rookie of the Year honors in 1984.

Davis forged another such season in 1987 after two so-so campaigns in 1985 and 1986; he hit .295 with 100 RBI and 86 runs scored, 29 homers, and 37 doubles. After another off-year in 1988 (although he again hit .295), Davis returned to form with a .305 batting average, 95 RBI, 21 homers, and 30 doubles in 1989.

His run production waned as the 1990s got underway, and though he was out of big-league ball after the 1992 season, Davis will always be a favorite with most Seattle fans.

Alvin Davis drops his bat and rushes for first base in a 1984 game.

DWIGHT GOODEN—NL 1984

Not since Tom Seaver dominated NL batters in the 1960s and 1970s had a Mets pitcher wowed the baseball world the way Dwight Gooden did in the 1980s. A power pitcher with a curveball that made grown men weep, Gooden burst upon the scene in 1984 as the Mets battled the Cubs for the division title. And even though the Mets failed in their bid to overtake the Cubs down the stretch, Gooden's rookie season was a stunner.

The nineteen-year-old kid went 17–9 with a 2.60 ERA and 276 strikeouts—tops in the majors that year and the record for rookie pitchers in this century. He allowed only 161 hits and 73 walks in 218 innings. The National League had several worthy candidates for Rookie of the Year honors in 1984—Orel Hershiser, Juan Samuel, and Gooden's teammate Ron Darling—but Gooden was, for many fans, the obvious choice. The BBWAA agreed. Gooden became the second consecutive Met to win the award.

Dwight Gooden winds up for a pitch in 1987.

Many a rookie flounders after putting together a solid debut season, but Dwight proved he was the real thing as soon as the 1985 season got underway.

Again, the Mets made a run at the division flag, and again they came up short (this time against the Cardinals), but Gooden himself was being mentioned in the same breath as Sandy Koufax, Bob Gibson, and Juan Marichal. He was also being mentioned in connection with the pitcher whose name graces the award for the year's top pitchers: Cy Young. And indeed, by year's end Dwight had fashioned one of the more awesome pitching ledgers of recent memory.

He won 24 games while losing just 4. He also pitched 16 complete games (8 of them shutouts); in 276-plus innings, he walked only 69 batters while striking out 268 and forging a 1.53 ERA. Gooden was the runaway winner of the NL Cy Young Award. His league-leading totals in wins, ERA, and strikeouts for 1985 gave him what is known as the pitcher's Triple Crown.

Although he has yet to approach those kinds of numbers again, "Doc" has nothing to prove to anyone regarding his abilities or accomplishments. He still displays flashes of his early brilliance despite arm and foot problems that have bothered him in recent years.

In 1987 Gooden underwent treatment for cocaine use; as part of the aftercare program, he agreed to submit to random drug testing. In late June of 1994, Major League Baseball suspended Gooden for sixty days for violating the aftercare program. When his 1994 suspension was announced, some sources reported that he had only missed a drug test; other sources reported that he had failed a random drug test, possibly two of them.

After going 3–4 in 1994, Dwight was found in violation of his aftercare program, and was suspended for the 1995 season. He signed on with the Yankees for the '96 season.

OZZIE GUILLEN—AL 1985

When people mention the name "Ozzie" on Chicago's South Side, you'd be right in thinking they're talking about a major league shortstop. But it's not the Cardinals' Ozzie Smith they're talking about; it's Ozzie Guillen of the White Sox.

Guillen was twenty-one when he debuted with the White Sox in 1985. He quickly established himself as a top-notch defensive player who could also make contact at the plate, bunt a runner over, and steal a base when the situation called for it. In 150 games, the native Venezuelan hit .273 with 21 doubles and 9 triples. Although he drove in only 33 runs, he scored 71 times.

But it was with his glove and his arm that Guillen wowed the fans and the media. He led AL shortstops in fielding percentage that first season, often making dazzling plays behind second and in the hole. He became a fan favorite for his hustle, his defense, and his upbeat nature. Ozzie was named the AL Rookie of the Year for 1985.

Guillen struggled at the plate in his second season, hitting only .250 in 159 games. He knocked in 14 more runs than he did in his rookie season, but his totals in doubles and runs scored were down.

Ozzie contributed much more with the bat during the 1987 campaign, hitting .279 with 51 RBI, 64 runs scored, 25 steals, 22 doubles, and 7 triples. He continues to impress people with his play at shortstop, too, especially his range and accurate throwing arm.

Guillen missed most of the 1992 season because of injuries received when he and Chicago left fielder Tim Raines collided in the outfield as they tried to catch a pop-up. Guillen came back strong in 1993, however, and was a major factor in the team's capture of the AL West Division flag.

Ozzie Guillen hit .288 in the strike-shortened 1994 season.

Vince Coleman—his name is synonymous with "steal."

VINCE COLEMAN—NL 1985

It was hero worship, pure and simple. Seven or eight children—all giggling and smiling and half-skipping, half-running—were trailing the young man through the lobby of the Holiday Inn. He was in street clothes, not in a baseball uniform, but the youngsters knew who he was. The young man laughed heartily as the little local autograph hounds formed a circle around him.

That's how it usually is for any young sports hero, but especially if you're Vince Coleman and two years earlier you set the rookie record for stolen bases in a season with 110.

When Coleman rewrote the record books in 1985, he also hit for a .267 average with 20 doubles and 10 triples. He scored 107 times and knocked in 40. For his efforts with the pennant-winning St. Louis Cardinals, Coleman was named the NL Rookie of the Year.

During the NL Championship series, Vince helped spark the Cardinals' comeback after being down, two games to none, to the Dodgers. The Cardinals went on to win the series, four games to two. But a freak accident—a 150-foot motorized device used to position the infield tarpaulin at Busch Stadium rolled over his left foot and up his leg as he trotted toward the Cardinals' dugout—prevented Coleman from playing in the World Series, which St. Louis lost to the cross-state Kansas City Royals.

Despite his league-leading 107 steals, Vince had an off-year at the plate in 1986; his .232 batting average and .304 on-base percentage in 600 at-bats were, by anyone's standards, a poor showing for a leadoff hitter. He did better during the 1987 season, however, hitting .289 with 109 steals and 121 runs scored and upping his on-base percentage by 60 points.

Vince signed with the New York Mets as a free agent after the 1990 season. His three subpar years in New York, which were marked by turmoil and controversy, ended midway through the 1993 season when the ballclub released him following an incident in Los Angeles in which Coleman was accused of throwing a lighted firecracker into a crowd of people and injuring a young child. Signing autographs for adoring youngsters in that Holiday Inn lobby seemed light-years away by then.

Coleman plied his trade with the Royals in 1994 and the Mariners in 1995.

JOSE CANSECO—AL 1986

Jose Canseco gets a hit in a 1987 game against the Royals.

Had the stolen base held greater importance in a team's arsenal in the 1950s, it's likely that Willie Mays or Mickey Mantle would have founded the "40-40 Club." But it was Jose Canseco in 1988 who became the first big-league player to steal as many as 40 bases and hit as many as 40 home runs in the same season.

He may never have another "career year" like that one, in which he hit .307 with 124 RBI to go with his 42 homers and 40 steals. But he will *certainly* never have another year like 1986, when he won the AL Rookie of the Year Award.

By then, the Oakland Athletics were fast becoming a powerhouse in the AL West, and Canseco was a major reason. Only twenty-one at the start of the 1986 season, Canseco quickly proved his value to the team. Although he wasn't always selective at the plate (he struck out 175 times that year and hit only .240), he powdered 33 balls over the fence and drove in 117 runs. He also hit 29 doubles, stole 15 bases, and scored 85 runs. Those are the kinds of numbers that win awards, and Canseco beat out several notable rivals for top rookie honors, including Wally Joyner, Ruben Sierra, and Cory Snyder.

In 1987 Jose put together a solid follow-up to his rookie campaign—he hit .257 with 31 homers, 35 doubles, 15 steals, 81 runs scored, and 113 RBI. He followed that with his 40-40 campaign in 1988 and an off-year in 1989, when he missed half the season because of a stress fracture in his left wrist, an injury he received during spring training. By season's end, Jose's health and timing had improved enough that he wound up with 17 homers and 57 RBI. In the 1989 World Series, Jose hit .357 with a homer and 3 RBI, but in the 1988 and 1990 Series, he made poor showings.

In 1990 Canseco put together another good season. His .274 batting average was complemented by 37 homers and 101 RBI. And in 1991, he nearly duplicated his 40-40 season of a few years before when he cracked 44 homers and stole 26 bases to go with his 122 RBI, 115 runs scored, and 32 doubles.

In August 1992, Canseco was traded to the Texas Rangers for outfielder Ruben Sierra and pitchers Bobby Witt and Jeff Russell. Jose showed he could also slug home runs in a Rangers uniform, and the fans at Arlington Stadium eventually accepted him as one of their own after rooting against him for several years. But during the 1993 season, Jose was placed on the team's disabled list when he suffered a career-threatening arm injury in a relief stint that saw him give up 2 hits, 3 walks, and 3 runs in an inning of work against the Boston Red Sox.

As a member of those same Red Sox, Jose rebounded nicely in 1994, hitting .282 with 31 homers and 90 RBI. He kept at it with a .306 batting average, 24 homers, and 81 RBI in 1995.

TODD WORRELL—NL 1986

Todd Worrell was nearly twenty-six when he debuted in a major league uniform. Agewise, that is getting up there for a rookie. But Worrell's timing was excellent, indeed, as he found himself part of the pennant-winning Cardinals of 1985.

But the following year was when Todd showed just how good he really was. With Bruce Sutter now wearing Atlanta Braves colors, Todd was the ace of the Cardinals' relief corps, and he forged a record-setting season for the defending NL champs. He saved 36 games—the major-league rookie-season record—and posted a 2.08 ERA with 73 strikeouts and just 86 hits in nearly 104 innings of work.

Worrell was named the National League's top rookie for 1986, beating out such future stars as Will Clark, Barry Bonds, and Barry Larkin for the honor. Todd became the second consecutive Redbird, after speedster Vince Coleman, to win the award.

In 1987 Worrell's ERA rose to 2.66, but he also accumulated three times as many strikeouts as walks in saving 33 games for the Cardinals as they made it to the World Series for the third time in the decade.

Todd was selected by the Cardinals in the first round of the June 1982 free-agent draft—he was among the first two dozen picks overall.

He was a starting pitcher for most of his minor league career. By 1985, however, he split his time between starting and relieving, and once the Cardinals organization moved him up to the big leagues, he was used solely as a reliever. From 1986 through 1989, Worrell saved a total of 121 games for St. Louis.

Todd's career, which since 1993 was being showcased in Los Angeles as a member of the Dodgers, has been interrupted by arm miseries. But his 1995 stats made it plain that he could still "bring it": a 4–1 record with a 2.02 ERA, 32 saves, and 61 strikeouts in 62 innings of relief.

Todd Worrell about to burn one past the enemy.

MARK McGWIRE—AL 1987

Mark McGwire sends a ball flying to the cheap seats. He did so 39 times in 1995.

Ruth and Gehrig, Maris and Mantle, Mays and McCovey, Aaron and Mathews, Santo and Williams—baseball history is filled with power-hitting duos that send opposing pitchers running for cover. In the mid- to late 1980s, the combination of Jose Canseco and Mark McGwire posed just such a threat to any hurler facing the Oakland A's lineup.

McGwire took the field with the A's during the dog days of 1986. Over the course of about 20 games, he hit a few home runs and plated a few runners, but there was little hint that 1987 would be an award-winning season for the rookie.

But what a season it was. McGwire poled a rookie-record 49 homers (which tied him with the Cubs' Andre Dawson for the major league lead), knocked in 118 runs and scored 97, and hit 28 doubles and 4 triples. He also hit .289 for the year and had a slugging percentage of .618, the AL record for rookies.

Mark was the easy winner in the AL Rookie of the Year balloting, and became the top home-run and RBI man in an A's lineup that was dubbed "the Bash Brothers by the Bay."

Canseco was second to McGwire in both home runs (31) and RBI (113). Together, they made an awesome combo at the plate; collectively, the A's starting lineup slugged 199 homers in 1987. Seven players were in double figures.

Like any power hitter worth his resin, Mark hit some tape-measure shots that put a charge into his teammates and a buzz into the crowd. Over the next three seasons, his home run totals were 32, 33, and 39, and his corresponding RBI totals were 99, 95, and 108. But with McGwire, it was either feast or famine, as he often struck out swinging and never came close to batting his rookie-year high of .289.

McGwire and his fans would just as soon forget 1991, when he hit an anemic .201 with 22 homers and a career-low 75 RBI. But Mark returned to terrorize AL pitchers in 1992, when he hit .268 with 42 homers and 104 RBI. He was injured for much of the 1993 season, playing in just 27 games, but he still hit .333 with 9 homers and 24 RBI. Mark's 1994 season ended in August, when he elected to have surgery to repair his left heel, which had hampered him for two years.

McGwire's hitting prowess has overshadowed his defensive skills, but Mark has improved steadily at first base since he entered the majors in 1986. He has a career fielding percentage of .994 and has led the league once each in putouts, assists, and total chances.

BENITO SANTIAGO—NL 1987

When the Florida Marlins signed free-agent catcher Benito Santiago in December 1992, the club signed a former NL Rookie of the Year and the man who holds the rookie-season record for most consecutive games batted safely (34).

They also signed a player who only once has put together a year as successful as his rookie season of 1987. At this point in his career, Santiago is struggling to regain that magic as a batsman. He may still have it in him to reach the lofty heights of his first full season.

In his rookie campaign with the Padres, Santiago hit an even .300 with 18 homers and 79 RBI. He also cracked 33 doubles, scored 64 times, and stole 21 bases. The only two negatives were his strikeout-to-walk ratio—112 to 16—and his 22 errors (the most for catchers in both leagues). But his bat-handling was more than enough to win him the 1987 NL Rookie of the Year Award.

Benito's second-best campaign came in 1991, when he hit .267 with 17 homers and a career-high 87 RBI. In 1992, he hit only .250 with 10 homers and 42 RBI; in 1993, he hit .230 with 13 homers and 50 RBI.

Santiago has fallen victim to injuries again and again throughout his career. He spent considerable time on the disabled list during the 1990 and 1992 seasons.

Benito hit .273 with 11 homers and 41 RBI as a Marlin in 1994, and .286 with 11 homers and 44 RBI with the Reds in 1995.

Benito Santiago about to dash for first base.

WALT WEISS—AL 1988

Until the 1993 season, the closest Walt Weiss had come to playing a full season was his rookie campaign of 1988. Injuries have dogged Weiss throughout his career, leaving him—and his fans—frustrated.

Weiss debuted in midseason of 1987, hitting a spectacular .462 in 16 games for the Oakland A's. He took over as the team's shortstop for the 1988 campaign. He hit .250 and chipped in with 39 RBI that year. He also hit 17 doubles and a trio each of triples and homers.

Despite the 15 errors he accumulated that season, Walt played well on defense, often dazzling the crowd with his ability to move laterally, snatch the ball in his glove, and throw it on the run to first base for the out. Weiss got the nod by the BBWAA as the AL's top rookie for 1988, becoming the third consecutive Oakland player to win the award.

Alternating between the A's roster, the disabled list, and the minor leagues for rehabilitation, Walt's next few seasons showed just how fragile a ballplayer's body can be when it suffers the injuries that his body did.

Even with his lack of playing time from one season to the next, Weiss has managed to play for two World Series teams, including the 1989 World Champion A's.

After the 1992 season, Walt was traded to the Florida Marlins, for whom he hit a career-best .266. He played for another expansion team—the Colorado Rockies—in 1994 and 1995.

A's shortstop Walt Weiss leaps over the Red Sox's Spike Owen as Owen slides past second base in the September 1, 1988, Oakland-Boston match-up.

CHRIS SABO—NL 1988

What does a .271 batting average with 40 doubles, 11 homers, 44 RBI, and 46 stolen bases get you? If you're Chris Sabo and the year is 1988, it gets you the NL Rookie of the Year Award as voted by the BBWAA.

In addition to his offensive numbers, Sabo fielded at a .966 clip for the season. He played nearly all his games at third base, but also took a couple of turns at shortstop. With his aggressive style of play, his hustle, and his occasional home-run power, it was evident from the start that Chris was going to be a big part of the Cincinnati Reds' resurgence in the coming years.

Sabo suffered a setback in 1989 when a knee injury forced him onto the disabled list and ate up half his season. For the year, he hit .260 with 21 doubles, 6 homers, and 29 RBI.

He roared back in 1990, though, hitting .270 with 71 RBI, 25 home runs, 38 doubles, and 25 stolen bases. He also scored 95 runs for a Reds team that won the NL pennant and a surprising four-game sweep of the A's in the World Series. In that Series, Sabo hit .563 and socked home runs in consecutive innings in Game Three.

Chris had an even more productive year at the plate during the 1991 season. He had career highs in batting average (.301), RBI (88), and home runs (26).

Another injury-riddled season followed in 1992, but in 1993 Sabo was once again producing at the plate with 82 RBI, 86 runs scored, 21 homers, and 33 doubles.

After the 1993 season, Chris signed a free-agent contract with the Orioles, but he was relegated to backup in favor of Leo Gomez. Still, in just 37 games in 1994, Chris poled 11 homers and knocked in 42 runs. In addition to playing third base, he worked the outfield and served as designated hitter. He hit .254 in limited action with the White Sox in 1995.

Chris Sabo, ready for action at the hot corner as the pitch is made.

GREGG OLSON—AL 1989

The Orioles knew exactly what they were getting when they selected Gregg Olson in the first round of the June 1988 free-agent draft: a cool customer on the mound.

And after only one full season under his belt, the talented young hurler proved that his supporters were not mistaken. Gregg set the AL rookie record for saves with 27. During that season he also fashioned a miniscule 1.69 ERA, and in 85 innings he gave up just 57 hits while striking out 90 batters. He won 5 and lost 2 and gave up only 1 home run all year.

Those would be impressive statistics for any reliever, but for an inexperienced pitcher who was not yet twenty-three years old, they are simply outstanding. Gregg was chosen as the league's top rookie for 1989, becoming only the second AL pitcher to win the award during the 1980s.

Olson wasted little time in showing everyone he was no one-season wonder. For his sophomore season, he saved 37 games, won 6, and compiled a 2.42 ERA. Again, his strikeout-to-walk ratio and his hits-to-innings-pitched ratio were very good. He forged similar numbers in saves and strikeouts in 1991, but his ERA rose to 3.18 and he allowed 74 hits in 74 innings.

Gregg enjoyed greater success in 1992, when he saved a career-high 36 games, lowered his ERA to 2.05, and improved on his strikeouts and hits per innings pitched.

In 1993 Olson was headed toward what looked like his first season of at least 40 saves when an elbow injury in August ended the season for him. He was signed by the Atlanta Braves for the 1994 season, but again found himself on the disabled list. For 1994, he went 0–2 with a 9.20 ERA and 1 save. He saved 3 games for K.C. in 1995.

What the batter sees when Gregg Olson readies a pitch.

JEROME WALTON—NL 1989

Jerome Walton was a fuel-injected center fielder when he broke camp with the Cubs in the spring of 1989. He was fast, he was daring, and he could catch the ball as well as he could hit it. Placed in the leadoff spot in the lineup, Walton sparked the Cubs offense like no player had since Bob Dernier in 1984.

But during a night game in early May, Walton tore a leg muscle while wheeling around the basepaths. He was placed on the disabled list for a month.

When he returned to the Cubs' lineup, Walton picked up where he left off: hitting, fielding, and running the bases in a blur.

He closed the season with a .293 batting average, 23 doubles, 46 RBI, and 64 runs scored to go with his 5 homers. He also stole 24 bases. In the field, he made just 3 errors all season. Walton became the first Cub since Billy Williams in 1961 to win the NL Rookie of the Year Award.

In the bitterly fought NL Championship series against the San Francisco Giants that October, Jerome hit .364, knocked in a pair of runs, and scored 4 times in a losing cause. He also played a flawless center field.

The 1990 season was a major disappointment for Walton. The young outfielder found himself on the disabled list twice—once with Chicago (for six weeks) and once with the Triple-A Iowa Cubs (for six more weeks). And although he did manage to squeeze a .263 average out of his bat, he was able to muster only 20 extra-base hits and steal just 14 bases.

Another rough go with the club in 1991 (a .219 batting average, 17 RBI, and 19 extra-base hits in 123 games) pushed him into the background, and after batting just .127 in limited action for the Cubs in 1992, Jerome was granted free agency at the end of that year.

He signed with the Angels, but the 1993 season saw him with nothing to show for his three plate appearances except a walk. His .309 and .290 batting averages for the Reds in 1994 and 1995, respectively, may be a sign of a comeback.

Jerome Walton connects in a May 1991 game against the Mets.

CHAPTER SIX

THE 1990s

SANDY ALOMAR JR.—AL 1990

Sandy Alomar Jr. gets ready to knock one out of the park.

Both his father and brother were infielders, but Sandy Alomar chose to ply his trade as a catcher. Of the three Alomars, he's the only one to win the Rookie of the Year Award. Now if he could just stay healthy for all of a few seasons, he might capitalize on the promise he showed in his rookie year.

"Junior" (his father is Sandy Alomar Sr. and his brother is Roberto Alomar) joined the San Diego Padres organization in 1983 but played in only eight games with the parent club through 1989, when the Padres traded him to the Cleveland Indians for Joe Carter. The Indians also got Chris James and All-Star second baseman Carlos Baerga in the deal.

While in the Padres' minor league system, Alomar had solid years at Triple-A Las Vegas in 1988 and 1989. For the 1989 campaign he hit .306 with 101 runs batted in, 13 homers, 33 doubles, 8 triples, and 88 runs scored. In both years he was named Pacific Coast League Player of the Year. But the Padres didn't need Sandy—they already had 1987 Rookie of the Year Benito Santiago firmly entrenched behind the plate.

After the trade to Cleveland, Alomar earned the starting catcher position with the Indians, and in 132 games he hit .290 with 66 RBI, 26 doubles, and 9 home runs. He also scored 60 runs and even stole 4 bases. Although he led AL catchers with 14 errors, he earned the coveted Gold Glove Award presented by Rawlings Sporting Goods. Sandy was named the AL Rookie of the Year for 1990, becoming the first Cleveland player to win the award since Joe Charboneau in 1980.

The 1991, 1992, and 1993 seasons were difficult ones for Sandy, as he fought the injury bug in each one. He played in only about 42 percent of his team's games during that stretch. Still, in the 64 games in which he appeared for the Indians in 1993, he managed to hit .270 with 6 homers and 32 RBI. For the 1994 season, Alomar hit .288 with 14 home runs and 43 RBI. He hit an even .300 for the AL champs in 1995.

DAVID JUSTICE—NL 1990

With six years of major league service under his belt, David Justice is hitting his stride.

The Atlanta Braves right fielder crushed 40 homers and knocked in 120 runs in 1993. Both totals were personal bests, and in combination with the power output of teammates Ron Gant, Fred McGriff, Terry Pendleton, and Jeff Blauser, it's easy to see why the 1993 Braves captured their third straight NL West title.

Justice's previous high in home runs was 28 in 1990, the year he hit .282 with 78 RBI, 76 runs scored, 23 doubles, and 11 stolen bases. That was also the year he won NL Rookie of the Year honors.

David has been a big reason for the franchise's recent resurgence after it snoozed through much of the 1980s. Following his impressive rookie season, he socked 21 homers in both 1991 and 1992 and played solid defense. In fact, those baseball fans who don't see a few Braves telecasts now and then may not be aware of how good Justice is at tracking down the fly balls that a lot of his peers would never reach. And his strong throws to the infield to cut down advancing runners have become his trademark.

The Braves selected Justice in the fourth round of the June 1985 free-agent draft. He didn't put up huge numbers in the minors, but the Braves organization kept the faith, and Justice has rewarded that faith many times over.

Despite consecutive World Series losses in 1991 and 1992, the disappointing outcome of the 1993 NL Championship series, and the strike-shortened 1994 season, the Braves will likely remain a contender for the next several years—in part because of the talent of players like David Justice. When the 1994 season abruptly ended in early August, Justice's numbers included 59 RBI, 19 homers, and a .313 batting average.

Although David's numbers were off during the regular season (his early-season shoulder injury was the root cause of his .253 BA and 78 RBI), he had a number of key hits that helped propel the Braves into postseason play. His solo homer was all Tom Glavine needed to win the sixth and final game of the 1995 Series.

David Justice smacks the ball off the middle of his bat in the May 22, 1993, match-up between the Braves and the Mets.

CHUCK KNOBLAUCH—AL 1991

Chuck Knoblauch had the kind of rookie season in 1991 that baseball-loving kids dream about having when they grow up.

The Twins had picked him in the first round of the June 1989 free-agent draft. After solid performances in their farm system, he was made their starting second baseman in 1991.

During the regular season, the young second baseman forged a .281 batting average with 50 RBI, 25 steals, 24 doubles, 6 triples, and 78 runs scored. He played well up the middle despite his 18 errors, and became an instant fan favorite in Minnesota's Hubert H. Humphrey Metrodome. His overall performance proved to be the winning ticket in the voting for the AL Rookie of the Year. He became the first Minnesota Twins player to capture the honor in more than a decade.

Then, in the AL Championship series, Chuck hit a cool .350 against the Toronto Blue Jays while playing a flawless second base. To top it all off, Chuck hit .308 in the World Series as the Twins prevailed over the Atlanta Braves in seven games. On defense, he divided his time between second base and shortstop.

Knoblauch came through for the Twins in his second year as well. He hit .297—16 points higher than his rookie-season average of .281—and improved his totals in RBI by 6, his runs scored by 26, and his stolen bases by 9. He also fared better in the field, cutting his errors by a two-thirds margin while increasing his total putouts by nearly 60.

In 1993 Chuck's offensive numbers slipped (.277, 41 RBI, 82 runs scored) but his 29 stolen bases led the team and his 27 doubles were a career high. In 1994 he made just 3 errors in 109 games, while hitting .312 and pounding 45 doubles. In 1995 he hit .333 with 34 doubles, 8 triples, and 11 home runs.

Chuck Knoblauch drops his bat and tears for first.

JEFF BAGWELL—NL 1991

No Houston Astros player had won the NL Rookie of the Year Award until Jeff Bagwell did it in 1991.

Bagwell, who was originally selected by the Boston Red Sox in the June 1989 free-agent draft but was traded to the Houston organization near the end of the 1990 season, had an immediate impact on the 1991 Astros' offense.

Jeff hit a robust .294 and his 82 RBI were fueled by his 15 homers, 26 doubles, and 4 triples. He also stole 7 bases and scored 79 runs. Jeff showed he was an able first baseman, too, making only 12 errors and fielding at a .991 clip for the season. Those were definitely top rookie numbers in the view of the BBWAA members.

Bagwell's batting average dropped 20 points the next year, but he improved in RBI (96), home runs (18), triples (6), doubles (34), steals (10), and runs scored (87). Jeff's eye at the plate also improved. He struck out nearly 20 fewer times than he did in 1991 while drawing 9 more walks.

That year, Bagwell also solidified his reputation as a steady defensive player: he made five fewer errors at first, substantially upped his totals in putouts and assists, and improved his fielding percentage to .995.

Jeff continues to improve with age. Only twenty-six years old as the 1994 season got into full swing, he wound up hitting .320 with 88 RBI, 20 homers, 13 steals, and 37 doubles—all career bests. Of course, Jeff might have done even better had he played a full season—in September of 1993 he was struck by an errant pitch that broke his left hand, effectively ending his season.

Bagwell not only made a comeback in 1994; he flourished. In just 400 at-bats, he accumulated a .368 batting average, a .750 slugging percentage, 104 runs scored, 32 doubles, 39 homers, and 116 RBI. He was also named the 1994 NL Most Valuable Player; he was the first Astro to win the award, and only the third NL player to be accorded the honor by unanimous vote.

Jeff Bagwell hit .290 with 21 homers in 1995.

PAT LISTACH—AL 1992

Injuries severely curtailed Pat Listach's sophomore campaign. He hit just .244 with 30 RBI, 50 runs scored, and 18 steals.

But when he is healthy, as he was in his rookie season of 1992, Pat is an exciting and productive player for the Milwaukee Brewers, who signed him in the free-agent draft of June 1988.

While he was in the minors, Listach gave no indication that he would be successful at the major league level. He often struggled at the plate and in the field, hardly the results that will impress big-league scouts. But Listach got his big-league chance as the 1992 season unfolded. He was the catalyst for a Brew Crew that nearly stole the AL East title from the Blue Jays in the last weekend of the season. Pat stole a club-record 54 bases, scored 93 runs, knocked in 47, and hit .290. For his role in Milwaukee's pennant drive, Listach was voted the AL Rookie of the Year.

Over the course of the 1993 season, Pat was hampered by injuries, and he ended that season with only a .244 batting average, 30 RBI, and 50 runs scored. He again spent a lot of time on the disabled list during the 1994 season; in 16 games, he hit .296 with 3 doubles and 2 RBI. In 1995, he hit only .219 with 10 extra-base hits in 59 games. Whether he will ever return to his rookie-season form remains to be seen.

Pat Listach will need new lumber after this swing.

ERIC KARROS—NL 1992

Once Eric Karros learns the strike zone a little better, many observers say, he will put together the kind of season that may win him NL Most Valuable Player honors. As it is, Karros has already won the league's Rookie of the Year Award, a feat he accomplished in 1992.

Eric was signed by the Los Angeles Dodgers organization in the June 1988 free-agent draft. In his four seasons in the minors, Karros never hit below .300 and was one of the top defensive first basemen no matter what league he played in.

During his debut season, Karros wasn't as selective at the plate as the Dodgers would have liked him to be—he struck out 103 times and walked only 37 times. And his .257 batting average was the lowest season total of his professional career.

But the young man proved he could drive in runs and hit with power, two qualities that will keep a player in the lineup regardless of his batting average. What's more, he played an outstanding first base for Los Angeles, fielding at a .993 clip for the year. Karros wound up winning the 1992 NL Rookie of the Year Award based on his 88 RBI, 20 homers, 30 doubles, and his strong defense.

Karros struggled through the early going of the 1993 campaign, but righted himself following the All-Star break and wound up with 80 RBI, 23 home runs, and 27 doubles for the season. His batting average for 1994 was only .247, but he reduced his strikeouts by more than 20 and put together a good (if not great) year, hitting .266 with 14 homers, 21 doubles, and 46 RBI. Perhaps the real Eric Karros took the field in 1995, when the first baseman was in double figures for home runs (32) and doubles (29), while hitting .298 with 105 RBI.

Eric Karros leaves his bat behind as he takes to the basepaths in the May 8, 1993, Dodgers-Giants game.

TIM SALMON—AL 1993

"Going into spring training, I wasn't trying to reach any marks," Tim Salmon told reporters after it was announced that the California Angels outfielder had been named the 1993 AL Rookie of the Year by the BBWAA. "I wanted to get my feet wet, get a rhythm going, get myself comfortable in the box every day," he said.

Salmon must have maintained a substantial comfort level from start to finish, as he hit .283 with 95 RBI while tying for the league mark in home runs with 31. He also hit 35 doubles and scored 93 runs. He may well have topped 100 in RBI and runs scored had he not suffered a broken finger with three weeks left in the season.

Salmon's reputation as a good hitter with decent defensive skills preceded him to the majors. With Edmonton of the Pacific Coast League in 1992, he hit a whopping .347 and led the league in RBI (105) and homers (29). He was up with the Angels late that season for the proverbial cup of coffee, but hit only .177 with a pair of homers and a half-dozen RBI.

He hit the ground running once the 1993 campaign got under way. And his selection as the league's best rookie player took on special significance: Tim became only the fourth AL rookie to win the award unanimously. If he stays healthy and learns to adapt to opposing pitcher's adjustments to his hitting style, Salmon is likely to be a central figure in the California Angels' pennant hopes for several years to come.

"Sophomore jinx"—baseball slang for a bad year after a player's successful rookie (or "freshman") year—didn't figure in Tim's 1994 campaign. He cracked 23 homers with 70 RBI while posting a .287 batting average. In fact, this is one Salmon that seems to get better with age: Tim reached his big-league career highs in batting average (.330), runs batted in (105), and home runs (34) in 1995.

Tim Salmon awaits the pitch.

MIKE PIAZZA—NL 1993

Nearly 1,400 young players were chosen before him in the June 1988 amateur draft, so observers could be forgiven for writing him off even before he pulled on his Dodgers uniform and stepped onto a major league field for the first time. And his so-so performance in 21 games for the Dodgers in 1992 did little to convince people that he would be anything more than a journeyman catcher. But slow-footed Mike Piazza knew in his heart that if he concentrated on being the best, he had the potential to make his mark in the bigs.

When the dust had settled at the end of the 1993 regular season, Mike had hammered out one of the greatest single-season performances by a rookie in baseball history. And indeed, Piazza not only won the NL Rookie of the Year Award, but won it unanimously—becoming the sixth NL rookie to do so.

Piazza's numbers for the 1993 season were incredible. He hit .318—the highest batting average for any NL rookie since the award went national in 1947—to go along with his 35 home runs, the most by an NL rookie since the 38 dingers slugged by the Reds' Frank Robinson in 1956. Piazza is the first NL rookie to knock in at least 100 runs for the season. (He drove in 112.)

Mike was so consistent throughout the 1993 campaign that, in the eyes of the fans and the media anyway, he was the odds-on favorite to win Rookie of the Year honors well before the season came to an end.

Not only were the Dodgers making a run at the pennant in 1994 when the strike dashed any hopes for postseason play, but Piazza's offensive output was again impressive: a .319 batting average with 24 homers and 92 RBI.

With nearly a full slate of games in 1995, Mike hit an eye-popping .346 with 32 homers and 93 RBI. These are the kinds of numbers that are getting him mentioned in the same breath as another Dodgers catcher—the great Roy Campanella.

Mike Piazza's hitting prowess has been well publicized, but the Dodgers catcher is an asset *behind* the plate as well.

BOB HAMELIN—AL 1994

Kansas City's power-hitting sensation, Bob Hamelin, hits the dirt.

Bob Hamelin was picked by the Kansas City Royals' farm system in the 1988 draft. About the only thing that kept him from reaching the majors sooner than he did was a back injury.

The club's brain trust called Bob up to the majors for the 1994 campaign, and he rewarded them with a .282 batting average, 25 doubles, 24 home runs, and 65 RBI for the strike-shortened season. In turn, the BBWAA voted him the AL Rookie of the Year, making him only the second Royals player to win the award (Lou Piniella was the first, twenty-five years earlier).

Hamelin was dubbed "Hammer" for pounding the ball into the outer reaches of AL ballparks, including a 440-foot blast against the Toronto Blue Jays' Dave Stewart. A few homers kept the Royals in the race for the AL Central title.

Generally regarded as the team's designated hitter, Bob also played two dozen games at first base. But it was his slugging, his hustle, and his on-field enthusiasm that the fans came to see, and Bob's 24-homer total was two better than the club's rookie record set by Bo Jackson in 1987.

Bob struggled in 1995. He divided his time between K.C.—where he hit .168 with 7 home runs and 25 RBI—and Triple A.

RAUL MONDESI—NL 1994

The Dodgers' minor league system has long been the envy of baseball, and Raul Mondesi is the latest reason for this envy.

In 1994 Mondesi hit .306, knocked in 56 runs, and socked 16 home runs, 8 triples, and 27 doubles. These were solid offensive numbers, and his defensive play was just as impressive: he committed only two errors in the outfield and he led the majors in assists with 16. The BBWAA made the native Dominican a unanimous choice for the 1994 NL Rookie of the Year Award, making him the second consecutive Dodger and the eleventh player overall to win unanimously. Raul was also the third consecutive Dodger rookie to win the award.

Baseball fans, Mondesi's teammates, and many of the Dodgers' opponents think Mondesi has the best outfield arm in baseball. With the combination of strength and accuracy in his throws from right field, it's hard to argue otherwise. Raul is being counted on to help lead the Dodgers to the postseason in the next several years. If his rookie season is any indication of what's to come, the rest of the NL better be ready for battle.

Raul's batting average dipped to .285 in 1995, but his production climbed to 88 RBI and 26 homers. He also cracked 23 doubles and 6 triples, and made 13 assists from the outfield.

Equally talented with glove or bat, Raul Mondesi is the Dodgers' seventh Rookie of the Year since 1979.

MARTY CORDOVA—AL 1995

Padres officials wanted Marty Cordova to one day play in San Diego, but the Las Vegas native elected not to sign with the organization in the free-agent draft of June 1987. The Padres' loss was a gain for the Minnesota Twins, with whom Cordova signed two years later: Cordova was named the 1995 AL Rookie of the Year by the BBWAA.

It took Marty a while to develop the skills that would lead him to the majors, but in 1992—his fourth year in the minors—he hit .341 and led the California League in runs batted in (131) and home runs (28). He was no slouch in the outfield, either, committing only 3 errors and making 10 assists. He was named the California League's Most Valuable Player for that year.

When he played for Nashville in the Southern League the following season, Marty's offensive numbers dropped sharply, but that didn't affect his fielding; he had the highest fielding percentage among the league's outfielders in 1993. Playing at the Triple-A level in Salt Lake in 1994, Marty's batting average shot up by more than 100 points over his 1993 average, to .358. His RBI total dropped to 66—half of his 1992 total—but he socked 19 homers, the second year in a row he hit that many.

Cordova was twenty-five at the start of the 1995 campaign, and he aged gracefully to twenty-six as the season progressed. For the year he batted .277 with 24 homers, 27 doubles, and 84 runs batted in.

It was the closest AL rookies race since 1979, when Toronto shortstop Alfredo Griffin and Twins third baseman John Castino tied for the top award. Cordova edged another rookie outfielder, California's Garret Anderson, for 1995 honors.

Marty told reporters that he used teammate Kirby Puckett's bats to achieve his first-year success, but added, "He gets a little better wood than I do." (Kirby hit .314 with 99 RBI, 23 homers, and 39 doubles.)

Minnesota's star rookie, Marty Cordova, heads for first base.

HIDEO NOMO—NL 1995

He speaks through an interpreter, but his onfield accomplishments are universally understood. The man in question is Hideo Nomo, freshman pitching sensation for the Los Angeles Dodgers who was named the National League's top rookie for 1995.

The twenty-seven-year-old Nomo accomplished a similar postseason feat in his native Japan in 1990 when he won the Rookie of the Year honors there. To win his Stateside award, Hideo led the National League with 236 strikeouts in 191 innings and posted a 13–6 record with a 2.54 ERA.

Although he failed to notch a victory after September 1, Nomo was overpowering the rest of the season. He pitched 5 scoreless innings in his big-league debut on May 2, won 7 consecutive games in June, and was named starter for the NL squad in the 1995 All-Star Game.

Hideo beat out slugging outfielder Chipper Jones of the Atlanta Braves in what some observers saw as an upset win. Jones hit .265 with 23 homers and 86 RBI.

Nomo became the fourth consecutive Dodger to win the league's top rookie honor, following in the footsteps of Eric Karros, Mike Piazza, and Raul Mondesi. And Nomo's award marked the second time in history that the Dodgers could boast of four straight years of having the league's best rookie.

Hideo Nomo shows the form that contributed to his sterling first year.

Rookies of the Year: A Comparison

The Baseball Writers' Association of America

In 1940 the Chicago chapter of the Baseball Writers' Association of America (BBWAA) established its Rookie of the Year Award. In 1947 the national organization assumed responsibility for awarding this honor. From 1940 through 1948, one award was presented. From 1949 to the present, two awards—one for each league—have been presented each year.

Year	Award Winner			
1940	AL	Lou Boudreau (SS), Cleveland Indians		
1941	NL	Pete Reiser (OF), Brooklyn Dodgers		
1942	NL	Johnny Beazley (P), St. Louis Cardinals		
1943	AL	Billy Johnson (3B), New York Yankees		
1944	NL	Bill Voiselle (P), New York Giants		
1945	AL	Dave Ferriss (P), Boston Red Sox		
1946	NL	Eddie Waitkus (1B), Chicago Cubs		
1947	NL	Jackie Robinson (1B), Brooklyn Dodgers		
1948	NL	Alvin Dark (SS), Boston Braves		
1949	AL	Roy Sievers (OF), St. Louis Brown	NL	Don Newcombe (P), Brooklyn Dodgers
1950	AL	Walt Dropo (1B), Boston Red Sox	NL	Sam Jethroe (OF), Boston Braves
1951	AL	Gil McDougald (3B-2B), New York Yankees	NL	Willie Mays (OF), New York Giants
1952	AL	Harry Byrd (P), Philadelphia Athletics	NL	Joe Black (P), Brooklyn Dodgers
1953	AL	Harvey Kuenn (SS), Detroit Tigers	NL	Jim Gilliam (2B), Brooklyn Dodgers
1954	AL	Bob Grim (P), New York Yankees	NL	Wally Moon (OF), St. Louis Cardinals
1955	AL	Herb Score (P), Cleveland Indians	NL	Bill Virdon (OF), St. Louis Cardinals
1956	AL	Luis Aparicio (SS), Chicago White Sox	NL	Frank Robinson (OF), Cincinnati Reds
1957	AL	Tony Kubek (OF-IF), New York Yankees	NL	Jack Sanford (P), Philadelphia Phillies
1958	AL	Albie Pearson (OF), Washington Senators	NL	Orlando Cepeda (1B), San Francisco Giants
1959	AL	Bob Allison (OF), Washington Senators	NL	Willie McCovey (1B), San Francisco Giants
1960	AL	Ron Hansen (SS), Baltimore Orioles	NL	Frank Howard (OF), Los Angeles Dodgers
1961	AL	Don Schwall (P), Boston Red Sox	NL	Billy Williams (OF), Chicago Cubs
1962	AL	Tom Tresh (SS OF), New York Yankees	NL	Ken Hubbs (2B), Chicago Cubs
1963	AL	Gary Peters (P), Chicago White Sox	NL	Pete Rose (2B), Cincinnati Reds
1964	AL	Tony Oliva (OF), Minnesota Twins	NL	Dick Allen (3B), Philadelphia Phillies
1965	AL	Curt Blefary (OF), Baltimore Orioles	NL	Jim Lefebvre (2B), Los Angeles Dodgers
1966	AL	Tommie Agee (OF), Chicago White Sox	NL	Tommy Helms (3B), Cincinnati Reds
1967	AL	Rod Carew (2B), Minnesota Twins	NL	Tom Seaver (P), New York Mets
1968	AL	Stan Bahnsen (P), New York Yankees	NL	Johnny Bench (C), Cincinnati Reds
1969	AL	Lou Piniella (OF), Kansas City Royals	NL	Ted Sizemore (2B), Los Angeles Dodgers
1970	AL	Thurman Munson (C), New York Yankees	NL	Carl Morton (P), Montreal Expos
1971	AL	Chris Chambliss (1B), Cleveland Indians	NL	Earl Williams (C), Atlanta Braves
1972	AL	Carlton Fisk (C), Boston Red Sox	NL	Jon Matlack (P), New York Mets
1973	AL	Al Bumbry (OF), Baltimore Orioles	NL	Gary Matthews (OF), San Francisco Giants
1974	AL	Mike Hargrove (1B), Texas Rangers	NL	Bake McBride (OF), St. Louis Cardinals
1975	AL	Fred Lynn (OF), Boston Red Sox	NL	John Montefusco (P), San Francisco Giants
1976	AL	Mark Fidrych (P), Detroit Tigers	NL	Pat Zachry (P), Cincinnati Reds Butch Metzger (P), San Diego Padres
1977	AL	Eddie Murray (1B), Baltimore Orioles	NL	Andre Dawson (OF), Montreal Expos
1978	AL	Lou Whitaker (2B), Detroit Tigers	NL	Bob Horner (3B), Atlanta Braves
1979	AL	Alfredo Griffin (SS), Toronto Blue Jays John Castino (3B), Minnesota Twins	NL	Rick Sutcliffe (P), Los Angeles Dodgers
1980	AL	Joe Charboneau (OF), Cleveland Indians	NL	Steve Howe (P), Los Angeles Dodgers
1981	AL	Dave Righetti (P), New York Yankees	NL	Fernando Valenzuela (P), Los Angeles Dodgers
1982	AL	Cal Ripken Jr. (SS-3B), Baltimore Orioles	NL	Steve Sax (2B), Los Angeles Dodgers
1983	AL	Ron Kittle (OF), Chicago White Sox	NL	Darryl Strawberry (OF), New York Mets
1984	AL	Alvin Davis (1B), Seattle Mariners	NL	Dwight Gooden (P), New York Mets
1985	AL	Ozzie Guillen (SS), Chicago White Sox	NL	Vince Coleman (OF), St. Louis Cardinals
1986	AL	Jose Canseco (OF), Oakland Athletics	NL	Todd Worrell (P), St. Louis Cardinals
1987	AL	Mark McGwire (1B), Oakland Athletics	NL	Benito Santiago (C), San Diego Padres
1988	AL	Walt Weiss (SS), Oakland Athletics	NL	Chris Sabo (3B), Cincinnati Reds
1989	AL	Gregg Olson (P), Baltimore Orioles	NL	Jerome Walton (OF), Chicago Cubs
1990	AL	Sandy Alomar Jr. (C), San Diego Padres	NL	David Justice (OF), Atlanta Braves
1991	AL	Chuck Knoblauch (2B), Minnesota Twins	NL	Jeff Bagwell (1B), Houston Astros
1992	AL	Pat Listach (SS), Milwaukee Brewers	NL	Eric Karros (1B), Los Angeles Dodgers
1993	AL	Tim Salmon (OF), California Angels	NL	Mike Piazza (C), Los Angeles Dodgers
1994	AL	Bob Hamelin (1B), Kansas City Royals	NL	Raul Mondesi (OF), Los Angeles Dodgers
1995	AL	Marty Cordova (OF), Minnesota Twins	NL	Hideo Nomo (P), Los Angeles Dodgers

The Sporting News

In 1946 the staff of *The Sporting News* established its Rookie of the Year Award. From 1946 through 1948 and in 1950, one award was presented. In 1949 and from 1951 through 1962, two awards—one for each league—were presented. From 1963 to the present, four awards—for the best rookie position player and the best rookie pitcher in each league—have been presented each year.

Year		Award Winner		
1946	NL	Del Ennis (OF), Philadelphia Phillies		
1947	NL	Jackie Robinson (1B), Brooklyn Dodgers		
1948	NL	Richie Ashburn (OF), Philadelphia Phillies		
1949	AL	Roy Sievers (OF), St. Louis Browns	NL	Don Newcombe (P), Brooklyn Dodgers
1950	AL	Whitey Ford (P), New York Yankees		
1951	AL	Minnie Minoso (OF), Chicago White Sox	NL	Willie Mays (OF), New York Giants
1952	AL	Clint Courtney (C), St. Louis Browns	NL	Joe Black (P), Brooklyn Dodgers
1953	AL	Harvey Kuenn (SS), Detroit Tigers	NL	Jim Gilliam (2B), Brooklyn Dodgers
1954	AL	Bob Grim (P), New York Yankees	NL	Wally Moon (OF), St. Louis Cardinals
1955	AL	Herb Score (P), Cleveland Indians	NL	Bill Virdon (OF), St. Louis Cardinals
1956	AL	Luis Aparicio (SS), Chicago White Sox	NL	Frank Robinson (OF), Cincinnati Reds
1957	AL	Tony Kubek (IF-OF), New York Yankees	NL	Ed Bouchee (1B), Philadelphia Phillies Jack Sanford (P), Philadelphia Phillies
1958	AL	Albie Pearson (OF), Washington Senators Ryne Duren (P), New York Yankees	NL	Orlando Cepeda (1B), San Francisco Giants Carlton Willey (P), Milwaukee Braves
1959	AL	Bob Alison (OF), Washington Senators	NL	Willie McCovey (1B), San Francisco Giants
1960	AL	Ron Hansen (SS), Baltimore Orioles	NL	Frank Howard (OF), Los Angeles Dodgers
1961	AL	Dick Howser (SS), Kansas City Royals Don Schwall (P), Boston Red Sox	NL	Billy Williams (OF), Chicago Cubs Ken Hunt (P), Cincinnati Reds
1962	AL	Tom Tresh (SS-OF), New York Yankees	NL	Ken Hubbs (2B), Chicago Cubs
1963	AL	Pete Ward (3B), Chicago White Sox Gary Peters (P), Chicago White Sox	NL	Pete Rose (2B), Cincinnati Reds Ray Culp (P), Philadelphia Phillies
1964	AL	Tony Oliva (OF), Minnesota Twins Wally Bunker (P), Baltimore Orioles	NL	Richie Allen (3B), Philadelphia Phillies Billy McCool (P), Cincinnati Reds
1965	AL	Curt Blefary (OF), Baltimore Orioles Marcelino Lopez (P), California Angels	NL	Joe Morgan (2B), Houston Astros Frank Linzy (P), San Francisco Giants
1966	AL	Tommie Agee (OF), Chicago White Sox Jim Nash (P), Kansas City Royals	NL	Tommy Helms (3B), Cincinnati Reds Don Sutton (P), Los Angeles Dodgers
1967	AL	Rod Carew (2B), Minnesota Twins Tom Phoebus (P), Baltimore Orioles	NL	Lee May (1B), Cincinnati Reds Dick Hughes (P), St. Louis Cardinals
1968	AL	Del Unser (OF), Washington Senators Stan Bahnsen (P), New York Yankees	NL	Johnny Bench (C), Cincinnati Reds Jerry Koosman (P), New York Mets
1969	AL	Carlos May (OF), Chicago White Sox Mike Nagy (P), Boston Red Sox	NL	Coco Laboy (3B), Montreal Expos Tom Griffin (P), Houston Astros
1970	AL	Roy Foster (OF), Cleveland Indians Bert Blyleven (P), Minnesota Twins	NL	Bernie Carbo (OF), Cincinnati Reds Carl Morton (P), Montreal Expos
1971	AL	Chris Chambliss (1B), Cleveland Indians Bill Parsons (P), Milwaukee Brewers	NL	Earl Williams (C), Atlanta Braves Reggie Cleveland (P), St. Louis Cardinals
1972	AL	Carlton Fisk (C), Boston Red Sox Dick Tidrow (P), Cleveland Indians	NL	Dave Rader (C), San Francisco Giants Jon Matlack (P), New York Mets
1973	AL	Al Bumbry (OF), Baltimore Orioles Steve Busby (P), Kansas City Royals	NL	Gary Matthews (OF), San Francisco Giants Steve Rogers (P), Montreal Expos
1974	AL	Mike Hargrove (1B), Texas Rangers Frank Tanana (P), California Angels	NL	Greg Gross (OF), Houston Astros John D'Acquisto (P), San Francisco Giants
1975	AL	Fred Lynn (OF), Boston Red Sox Dennis Eckersley (P), Cleveland Indians	NL	Gary Carter (OF-C), Montreal Expos John Montefusco (P), San Francisco Giants
1976	AL	Butch Wynegar (C), Minnesota Twins Mark Fidrych (P), Detroit Tigers	NL	Larry Herndon (OF), San Francisco Giants Butch Metzger (P), San Diego Padres
1977	AL	Mitchell Page (OF), Oakland Athletics Dave Rozema (P), Detroit Tigers	NL	Andre Dawson (OF), Montreal Expos Bob Owchinko (P), San Diego Padres
1978	AL	Paul Molitor (2B), Milwaukee Brewers Rich Gale (P), Kansas City Royals	NL	Bob Horner (3B), Atlanta Braves Don Robinson (P), Pittsburgh Pirates
1979	AL	Pat Putnam (1B), Texas Rangers Mark Clear (P), California Angels	NL	Jeff Leonard (OF), Houston Astros Rick Sutcliffe (P), Los Angeles Dodgers
1980	AL	Joe Charboneau (OF), Cleveland Indians Britt Burns (P), Chicago White Sox	NL	Lonnie Smith (OF), Philadelphia Phillies Bill Gullickson (P), Montreal Expos
1981	AL	Rich Gedman (C), Boston Red Sox Dave Righetti (P), New York Yankees	NL	Tim Raines (OF), Montreal Expos Fernando Valenzuela (P), Los Angeles Dodgers
1982	AL	Cal Ripken Jr. (SS-3B), Baltimore Orioles Ed Vande Berg (P), Seattle Mariners	NL	Johnny Ray (2B), Pittsburgh Pirates Steve Bedrosian (P), Atlanta Braves
1983	AL	Ron Kittle (OF), Chicago White Sox Mike Boddicker (P), Baltimore Orioles	NL	Darryl Strawberry (OF), New York Mets Craig McMurtry (P), Atlanta Braves
1984	AL	Alvin Davis (1B), Seattle Mariners Mark Langston (P), Seattle Mariners	NL	Juan Samuel (2B), Philadelphia Phillies Dwight Gooden (P), New York Mets
1985	AL	Ozzie Guillen (SS), Chicago White Sox Teddy Higuera (P), Milwaukee Brewers	NL	Vince Coleman (OF), St. Louis Cardinals Tom Browning (P), Cincinnati Reds
1986	AL	Jose Canseco (OF), Oakland Athletics Mark Eichhorn (P), Toronto Blue Jays	NL	Robby Thompson (2B), San Francisco Giants Todd Worrell (P), St. Louis Cardinals
1987	AL	Mark McGwire (1B), Oakland Athletics Mike Henneman (P), Detroit Tigers	NL	Benito Santiago (C), San Diego Padres Mike Dunne (P), Pittsburgh Pirates
1988	AL	Walt Weiss (SS), Oakland Athletics Bryan Harvey (P), California Angels	NL	Mark Grace (1B), Chicago Cubs Tim Belcher (P), Los Angeles Dodgers
1989	AL	Craig Worthington (3B), Baltimore Orioles Tom Gordon (P), Kansas City Royals	NL	Jerome Walton (OF), Chicago Cubs Andy Benes (P), San Diego Padres
1990	AL	Sandy Alomar Jr. (C), Cleveland Indians Kevin Appier (P), Kansas City Royals	NL	David Justice (OF), Atlanta Braves Mike Harkey (P), Chicago Cubs
1991	AL	Chuck Knoblauch (2B), Minnesota Twins Juan Guzman (P), Toronto Blue Jays	NL	Jeff Bagwell (1B), Houston Astros Al Osuna (P), Houston Astros
1992	AL	Pat Listach (SS), Milwaukee Brewers Cal Eldred (P), Milwakee Brewers	NL	Eric Karros (1B), Los Angeles Dodgers Tim Wakefield (P), Pittsburgh Pirates
1993	AL	Tim Salmon (OF), California Angels Aaron Sele (P), Boston Red Sox	NL	Mike Piazza (C), Los Angeles Dodgers Kirk Rueter (P), Montreal Expos
1994	AL	Bob Hamelin (1B), Kansas City Royals Brian Anderson (P), California Angels	NL	Raul Mondesi (OF), Los Angeles Dodgers Steve Trachsel (P), Chicago Cubs
1995	AL	Garret Anderson (OF), California Angels Julian Tavarez (P), Cleveland Indians	NL	Chipper Jones (3B), Atlanta Braves Hideo Nomo (P), Los Angeles Dodgers

Bibliography

Broeg, Bob. *The Man Stan...Musial Then and Now.* St. Louis: The Bethany Press, 1977.

Cohen, Richard M., and David S. Neft. *The World Series.* New York: Macmillan Publishing Co., 1986.

Craft, David, and Tom Owens. *Redbirds Revisited.* Chicago: Bonus Books, Inc., 1990.

Hoppel, Joe, ed. *The Sporting News Official Baseball Guide—1984.* St. Louis: The Sporting News Publishing Company, 1984.

Meserole, Mike, ed. *The 1994 Information Please Sports Almanac.* Boston: Houghton Mifflin Company, 1994.

Reichler, Joseph L. *The Baseball Record Companion.* New York: Collier Books, 1987.

The staff of *The Sporting News. Daguerrotypes.* St. Louis: The Sporting News Publishing Company, 1990.

Thorn, John, and Pete Palmer, eds., with David Reuther. *Total Baseball.* New York: Time Warner Books, 1991.

Tygiel, Jules. *Jackie Robinson and His Legacy.* New York: Vintage Books, 1984.

White, Paul, and the staff of *Baseball Weekly: Baseball Weekly 1994 Almanac.* Arlington, Va.: Gannet Co. Inc., 1994.

Williams, Ted, with John Underwood. *My Turn at Bat.* New York: Fireside Books, 1988.

Index